THE KILLING
—of—
UNCLE SAM

THE DEMISE OF THE UNITED STATES OF AMERICA

STUDY GUIDE

This study guide is the ultimate companion workbook that provides readers with an in-depth synopsis of the book, *The Killing of Uncle Sam: The Demise of the United States of America*. *The Killing of Uncle Sam* by River Publishing is available on Amazon.com, BarnesandNoble.com and fine bookstores everywhere.

RODNEY HOWARD-BROWNE *and* **PAUL L. WILLIAMS**

River Publishing

CONTENTS

Prologue: Killing Uncle Sam vii

PART ONE: OUT OF AFRICA 1

1   The Vision of a Freemason 3

2   The African Hell-hole 6

3   Meeting Rothschild 9

4   The Lure of the Occult 14

5   Boers and Blood 17

6   So Little Done, So Much to Do 21

PART TWO: THE NEW WORLD 25

7   Converting Carnegie 27

8   The Rise of Foundations 30

9   New American Pilgrims 33

10 The Duck Hunters 36

11 "Control of the World" 40

PART THREE: WAR TO END ALL WARS 45

12 The Serpent's Egg 47

13 Making Hay 50

14 Peace and Punishment 54

PART FOUR: THE AMERICAN ESTABLISHMENT 59

15 The Shadow Government 61

16 A Designed Depression 67

17 The Police State 71

PART FIVE: THE OCCULT ECONOMY 75

18   Confiscated Gold 77

19   The Mother Bank 80

20   The Mother Boxes 84

PART SIX: THE BREAKING OF NATIONS 87

21   The Problem with Hitler 89

22   Baiting Nazis and "Nips" 93

23   The Secret Army 98

24   Producing the Plague 102

PART SEVEN: ENDLESS ENTANGLEMENTS 107

25   A Cancerous Growth 109

26   The Evil Sisters 114

27   The Bastard Son 122

28   Onslaught of Atrocities 127

PART EIGHT: THE POINT OF NO RETURN 133

29   The New Frontier 135

30   A Hell of a Hoax 141

31   The Black Bank 146

PART NINE: THE FINAL CURTAIN 151

32   Transforming the Population 153

33   Only the Dead Know Brooklyn and Other Stories 160

34   The New Network 166

35   The Globalization of Poverty 176

PART TEN: AMERICA, NO MORE 181

36   The Road to 9/11 183

37   The Mysteries of 9/11 191

38   War Without End 197

39   After the Funeral 208

Epilogue: Raising the Dead 214

Notes 226

PROLOGUE

KILLING UNCLE SAM

1. Nation comes from the Latin word *nascere*, which means "to be born."

2. A nation is organic. It is born. It develops. And it dies.

3. A nation is a place defined by borders. It is inhabited by people who share the same language, culture, history, and heritage.

4. America was formed by immigrants from Western Europe who were bonded by basic political and religious beliefs.

5. As a nation, America was personified by Uncle Sam, a character developed by Samuel Wilson during the War of 1812.

The Constitution of the United States of America
Written in 1787 by James Madison, it is the supreme law of the United States of America. The Constitution's first three words are: "We the People," which affirms that the government of the United States exists to serve its citizens.

6. Over the course of the 19ᵗʰ century, Uncle Sam came to resemble Andrew Jackson, the rough and tumble president who abolished America's first national bank.

7. Americans developed into a distinctive and easily identifiable race.

8. The killing of Uncle Sam was planned by a cabal of globalists in England.

9. The process of the killing was slow and painful, entailing the creation of the Federal Reserve System, the Council on Foreign Relations, the United Nations, the World Bank, the International Monetary Fund, and the World Trade Organization.

10. The killing was, in part, accomplished by opening America's borders to the Third World so that the nation would lose its distinctive character and culture.

DISCUSSION

A. Is nationalism an outgrowth of an ideology? Why? Why not?

_____

_____

_____

_____

B. Provide examples of the resurgence of tribalism in the 21ˢᵗ century.

_____

_____

_____

_____

PROLOGUE: KILLING UNCLE SAM

C. Discuss the development of Creedalism in contemporary political thought.

_____

_____

_____

_____

D. How is it possible to kill a nation?

_____

_____

_____

_____

E. How did the character of Uncle Sam come to exemplify America?

_____

_____

_____

_____

PART ONE

OUT OF AFRICA

"When we get piled upon one another in large cities, as in Europe, we shall become as corrupt as Europe."
—THOMAS JEFFERSON

"The real menace of our Republic is the invisible government which like a giant octopus sprawls its slimy legs over our cities, states and nation."
—MAYOR (1918-1925) JOHN F. HYLAN OF NEW YORK.

President Franklin Roosevelt said this on November 21, 1933: "The real truth of the matter is, as you and I know, that a financial element in the larger centers has owned the government since the days of Andrew Jackson."

1

THE VISION OF A FREEMASON

1. In 1877, Cecil Rhodes conceived of a one world order that would be controlled by an elite group of wealthy businessmen, bankers, and politicians.

2. His notion of this new order was rooted in Freemasonry.

3. Freemasonry was created by a group of British aristocrats who gathered at a London ale house in 1716.

4. The Freemasons based their society on the teachings of Gnosticism, considered an ancient Judeo-Christian heresy.

5. Gnosticism affirms that the highest god is a being of immeasurable light. A spark of this light is encased in every human soul.

Cecil Rhodes
Rhodes received his vision of a New World Order on the very day that he underwent the initiation rite of freemasonry in which he was pledged to serve as a light bearer.

6. Man, according to Gnosticism, remains enslaved by a lesser deity or "demiurge," who is the God of the Old Testament.

7. In Gnosticism, a man can only escape from the tyranny of the demiurge by undergoing several stages or "degrees" of enlightenment.

8. Those who reach the highest degree of enlightenment realize that the highest god is Lucifer, the light bearer.

9. Freemasonry, like Gnosticism, espouses a system of beliefs that can be embraced by individuals of all religious persuasions.

10. For Rhodes, religious unification under the precepts of Freemasonry would constitute the first step toward world government.

11. Rhodes believed that the unification of the world had been made possible by the industrial revolution.

12. Rhodes believed that the English represented a master race that had been earmarked to rule the world by the process of natural selection.

DISCUSSION

A. Rhodes was not the only 19th-century figure to advance the concept of a New World Order. Karl Marx was also a utopian who set about to create a universal system of government. Discuss the similarities and differences between Rhodes and Marx.

B. Freemasonry is generally presented as a benign society that poses no threat to the existing order of things. Is Freemasonry really a harmless fraternity? What political, cultural, and religious upheavals were caused by Freemasonry?

_____

_____

_____

_____

C. Discuss the notion of a master race. How is genetics integral to the creation of a New World Order?

_____

_____

_____

_____

D. Why was free trade the central concern of Cecil Rhodes?

_____

_____

_____

_____

2

THE AFRICAN HELL-HOLE

1. Rhodes made his vast fortune from the diamond mines in Kimberley, South Africa.

2. At Oxford, Rhodes was greatly influenced by the writings of John Ruskin, who maintained that Britain's destiny was to rule the world.

3. Ruskin advocated the institution of global socialism, a teaching that Rhodes embraced.

4. Rhodes believed that the first step toward the creation of a new world order was the conquest of the vast continent of Africa which possessed a bounty of natural resources.

5. In 1877, Rhodes returned to South Africa, where he set up his "band of brothers."

6. The band of brothers was encouraged to use their vast wealth to expand the British Empire.

7. The brothers were to avoid all emotional entanglements, including marriage.

DISCUSSION

A. Why was the conquest of Africa so important?

_____

_____

_____

_____

B. How did homosexuality come to play a major part in the establishment of Rhodes's secret society?

_____

_____

_____

_____

C. Why are diamonds, which are plentiful in various parts of the world, considered precious?

_____

_____

_____

_____

D. Discuss the influence of John Ruskin on 19th-century political philosophy.

_____

_____

_____

_____

E. What were the common characteristics of the band of brothers?

_____

_____

_____

_____

3

MEETING ROTHSCHILD

1. In 1888, Rhodes met Lord Nathan Rothschild to secure funding for his attempt to purchase all the diamond mines in South Africa.

2. The Rothschild family had complete control of the Bank of England, which regulated the nation's currency.

3. The Rothschilds had developed fractional banking and the concept of fiat money.

4. In America, the Rothschild family had been the principal shareholders of the First and Second Banks of America, which were centralized institutions that regulated the new nation's economy.

Nathan Rothschild
"I care not what puppet is placed on the throne of England to rule the Empire. The man who controls Britain's money supply controls the British Empire and I control the British money supply."—Nathan Mayer Rothschild

5. The Rothschilds were routed from America by Andrew Jackson, who dismantled the central bank and deposited the country's money in state banks.

6. Despite the setback in America, the Rothschilds continued their global expansion by establishing financial ties to such countries as Austria, Germany, Russia, Italy, France, Egypt, South Africa, China, India, New Zealand and Australia.

7. The Rothschilds established close relations with other Jewish banking families, including the Cohens, Warburgs, Schiffs, Kuhns, Loebs, Lazards, Lehmans, and Goldmans. These families worked together, shared resources, and engaged in joint business ventures.

8. By November 1888, the relationship between Cecil Rhodes and Nathan Rothschild had grown so close that Rhodes drafted a new will in which he named Rothschild the sole beneficiary of his estate.

9. Rothschild used the wealth accumulated by Rhodes to establish a British secret society as a counterpart to the band of brothers that Rhodes had set up in South Africa. The British secret society, which Rhodes dubbed "the Society of the Elect," was to be modeled after the Society of Jesus, which St. Ignatius Loyola had established in 1544.

10. Rothschild attracted a host of influential aristocrats to the "Society of the Elect," including Lord Reginald Baliol Brett, Queen Victoria's closest advisor; Lord Archibald Primrose, the 5th Earl of Rosebery and Rothschild's son-in-law, who would serve as Britain's prime minister from 1894 to 1895; and Arthur James Balfour, 1st Earl of Balfour, who would become the British prime minister from 1902 to 1905.

11. Rhodes's ties to these aristocrats would become tightened by their shared homosexuality and their preference for "burly, blue-eyed boys."

12. Among Rothschild's other recruits to the Society were Albert Lord Grey and Robert Armstrong Yates, two prominent members of the British Parliament; William Palmer, the 2ⁿᵈ Earl of Selborne; and Alfred Milner, under-secretary of finance in Egypt.

DISCUSSION

A. How did the House of Rothschild gain a stranglehold on the economy of the British Empire?

_____

_____

_____

_____

B. Discuss the role of the Rothschilds in the creation of modern banking.

_____

_____

_____

_____

C. Discuss the early history of centralized banking in America.

_____

_____

_____

_____

D. Why did Andrew Jackson view the central bank as the greatest threat to American democracy?

_____

_____

_____

_____

E. How did the vision of Cecil Rhodes coincide with the agenda of the Rothschild family?

_____

_____

_____

_____

F. What is real wealth? How is it accumulated?

_____

_____

_____

_____

G. Discuss the pivotal importance of the partnership between Rhodes and Rothschild on the course of human history.

_____

_____

_____

_____

A MARRIAGE MADE IN HELL

Rothschild granted Rhodes the financial means to purchase all the diamond mines in Kimberley, South Africa and to set up DeBeers, a corporation that maintains control of the diamond industry. In turn, Rhodes granted Rothschild the political means to gain control of the world's economy, including the means to establish another central bank in America.

4

THE LURE OF THE OCCULT

1. During his visit to England in 1889, Rhodes recruited William T. Stead, a noted journalist, to join the Society of the Elect.

2. Rhodes and Stead established the structure of the Society as a series of concentric circles.

3. Rhodes attracted more recruits, including Cardinal Henry Edward Manning, the leading Roman Catholic prelate in England, and William Booth, the founder of The Salvation Army.

4. The members of the Society of the Elect shared much in common. They were Masons, ardent British imperialists, Social Darwinists, and men of power and means with close ties to the Rothschild family.

William T. Stead
emerged as a leading character in the saga of the Society of the Elect.

5. The members also shared an interest in the occult, including the works of Helena Petrovna Blavatsky, a noted Satanist.

6. The members believed that supernatural assistance was required to create the New World Order.

DISCUSSION

A. What were the common characteristics of the members of the Society of the Elect?

_____

_____

_____

_____

B. Discuss the ties of Freemasonry to Luciferianism.

_____

_____

_____

_____

C. Why were the shelves of the private library of Cecil Rhodes lined with the works of Helena Petrovna Blavatsky?

_____

_____

_____

_____

D. Explain the connection between Blavatsky and the Lucan Trust, the official publishing arm of the United Nations.

_____

_____

_____

_____

E. Discuss the development of the Society of the Elect's circles within circles into a covert system of international government.

_____

_____

_____

_____

F. Discuss the religious beliefs of Cecil Rhodes and other members of the Society of the Elect.

_____

_____

_____

_____

G. Explain the ties between Rhodes and William Booth. How is this relationship mirrored in modern American political history?

_____

_____

_____

_____

5

BOERS AND BLOOD

1. In 1891, Rhodes became Prime Minister of the Cape Colony, a position he would hold for the next five years.

2. To unify the vast continent into one enormous country, Rhodes laid plans for a railroad from Cairo to Cape Town.

3. But before this venture got underway, matters within the Cape Colony remained to be settled. The discovery of seemingly limitless gold reserves in Witwatersrand brought thousands of "Uitlanders" ("foreigners") to the Transvaal, which remained under the rule of the "Boers" (Dutch settlers). The foreigners, for the most part, came from Great Britain, Australia, and the United States. Few spoke Dutch or German, the

Leander Starr Jameson
was Cecil Rhodes's right-hand man. He conducted the Jameson Raid that brought about the Second Boer War.

dominant European languages in the Transvaal and the Orange Free State, and they were subjected to restrictions, including the requirement of a four-year residency in the Boer territories before one would be granted the right to vote in public elections.

4. Rhodes, believing that the situation in Johannesburg was on the verge of armed insurrection, organized an invasion of the Boer Republic under Sir Leander Starr Jameson.

5. The raid was a debacle, but it produced an important blowback. Kaiser Wilhelm of Germany sent a telegram to Paul Kruger, the president of the Transvaal, in which he congratulated Kruger for killing English settlers without mentioning a word about the plight of the Uitlanders.

6. The telegram inflamed the British people, who then decided to come to the aid of the Uitlanders. The presence of British troops on the border of the Boer Republic gave rise to the Second Boer War.

7. By the time the conflict came to an end in 1902, 7,582 British soldiers had been killed in action, 13,139 had died of disease, 40,000 had been wounded, and one had been eaten by a crocodile. Six thousand Boers were killed in action, while 26,000 white civilians and 17,182 African natives died of disease and starvation in concentration camps that had been set up in the Cape and Orange River colonies.

8. The war led to the annexation of the Transvaal and the Orange Free State into the British Empire. The New World Order was coming into existence.

DISCUSSION

A. Why was the Second Boer War necessary for the establishment of a New World Order?

_____

_____

_____

_____

B. How did the Second Boer War pave the way for World War I?

_____

_____

_____

_____

C. Discuss the role of genocide in paving the way for internationalism.

_____

_____

_____

_____

D. How did the Second Boer War benefit the Society of the Elect and pave the way for a New World Order?

_____

_____

_____

_____

E. What were the benefits of the Second Boer War for the British Empire?

_____

_____

_____

_____

F. Discuss the impact of the Second Boer War upon the Society of the Elect.

_____

_____

_____

_____

6

SO LITTLE DONE, SO MUCH TO DO

1. During his final years, Rhodes realized that the United States, rather than Great Britain, should assume the leading role in forging the New World Order.

2. After Rhodes died in 1902, Lord Alfred Milner assumed leadership of the Society of the Elect, which he renamed "The Roundtable."

3. Milner recruited numerous statesmen, bankers, and aristocrats to the secret society, including Sir Patrick Duncan, Philip Henry Kerr, 1st Baron Robert Henry Brand, Lionel Curtis, George Geoffrey Dawson, John Buchan, T. E. Lawrence, Leo Amery, Stanley Baldwin, Sir Edward Peacock, and Rudyard Kipling.

4. Milner sent members of the Roundtable to the United States, Canada, Australia, New Zealand, and British colonies throughout the world to attract influential new members to the secret society so that the dream of Rhodes could come to fruition.

5. As High Commissioner for South Africa and the 1st Governor of the Transvaal and Orange River Colony, Milner remained a Rothschild lackey and managed the Roundtable in accordance with the directives of the Rothschild family.

6. Along with Rothschild, Milner established the Rhodes Scholarships at Oxford University. The scholarships were granted to "young colonists" with the purpose of "instilling into their minds the advantages of the colonies as well as to England for the retention of the Unity of the Empire."

7. American scholars received the lion's share of the scholarships. At the completion of their two years at Oxford, these scholars were to return to the United States so they could obtain prominent positions in academics, politics and the media. In this way, they could serve to undermine the nation's sovereignty. As soon as the Rhodes Fund was established, massive amounts of money poured into its coffers from the estate of Alfred Beit, the Carnegie United Kingdom Trust, and organizations associated with J.P. Morgan and John D. Rockefeller.

DISCUSSION

A. Discuss the evolution of the Society of the Elect into the Roundtable Movement.

_____

_____

_____

_____

B. What part did the Rhodes Scholarships play in the formation of a New World Order?

_____

_____

_____

_____

C. Discuss the role of Alfred Milner in the formation of a global shadow government.

_____

_____

_____

_____

D. Explain the importance of Africa to the New World Order.

_____

_____

_____

_____

PART TWO

THE NEW WORLD

"Some of the biggest men in the United States, in the field of commerce and manufacture, are afraid of something. They know that there is a power somewhere so organized, so subtle, so watchful, so interlocked, so complete, so pervasive, that they had better not speak above their breath when they speak in condemnation of it."
—WOODROW WILSON

"The democracy will cease to exist when you take away from those who are willing to work and give to those who would not."
—THOMAS JEFFERSON

"The world is governed by very different personages from what is imagined by those who are not behind the scenes."
—ENGLISH PRIME MINISTER BENJAMIN DISRAELI, IN 1844.

7

CONVERTING CARNEGIE

1. In 1900, Andrew Carnegie was the richest man in America.

2. Carnegie possessed close ties to William Stead and other members of Rhodes's Society of the Elect and became imbued with Rhodes's vision of a New World Order.

3. Although Carnegie never met Rhodes, the two men shared much in common. They were Freemasons, ardent Anglophiles, and agnostics, who espoused universal socialism. They also possessed enormous wealth and an interest in the occult.

4. Carnegie built The Hague in the Netherlands so that mankind could be ruled by a single system of justice, and promoted the idea of a League of Nations.

5. Carnegie was socially and financially allied to J.P. Morgan, who purchased U.S. Steel from him. The interests of the two industrialists were so intertwined that it was impossible to separate them.

DISCUSSION

A. How did Andrew Carnegie become imbued with the vision of Cecil Rhodes?

_____

_____

_____

_____

B. Discuss the strategic role Carnegie played in the formation of international law and government.

_____

_____

_____

_____

C. Discuss the ties of Carnegie to the House of Rothschild.

_____

_____

_____

_____

D. How did the business and political interests of Carnegie and J.P. Morgan become intertwined?

_____

_____

_____

_____

E. Discuss the religious beliefs of Andrew Carnegie.

_____

_____

_____

_____

8

THE RISE OF FOUNDATIONS

1. By 1905, the Carnegie Foundation for the Advancement of Teaching (CFAT) gained control of America's educational system.

2. CFAT promoted socialism, agnosticism, and globalism. Institutions of higher learning throughout the country came to rely on CFAT for funding.

3. In order to receive funding, the institutions had to comply with CFAT's principles.

4. John D. Rockefeller, impressed by CFAT, established the General Education Board (GEB), which standardized the curricula in America's high schools.

5. Thanks to CFAT and GEB, American history was rewritten, and the content of textbooks controlled and censored.

Andrew Carnegie
Since Carnegie was an avowed socialist, an agnostic, a globalist, and an associate of the Rhodes Society, universities throughout America began to reflect his ideology and beliefs. Carnegie was seeking control of the American political and education systems to further a New World Order.

6. Through his foundations, Rockefeller provided benefactions to America's leading seminaries that began to promote the concept of a one-world religion.

7. Within these seminaries, the gospel of Jesus Christ was "demythologized" and stripped of all "theological accretions, including the Virgin Birth, the miracles, and the Resurrection," so that the "kergyma" or "original message" of the historic Jesus could recaptured for modern man.

DISCUSSION

A. Discuss the key role of foundations in the formation of a shadow government.

_____

_____

_____

_____

B. How did education become standardized in the United States?

_____

_____

_____

C. Discuss the role of foundations in the rewriting of American history.

_____

_____

_____

_____

D. What role did the foundations play in the development of mainstream religion?

_____

_____

_____

_____

E. How do non-profit foundations continue to control the American educational, cultural, and political systems?

_____

_____

_____

_____

F. What role did the foundations play in the development of the U.S.'s foreign entanglements?

_____

_____

_____

_____

9

NEW AMERICAN PILGRIMS

1. J.P. Morgan assumed the task of creating a secret society in America to advance the goals of Cecil Rhodes.

2. Like Carnegie, Rhodes, and members of the Society of the Elect, J.P. Morgan was extremely wealthy, an ardent Anglophile, a Freemason, and a practitioner of the occult.

3. Through his business connection with Lord Nathan Rothschild, Morgan became acquainted with members of the Society of the Elect, including Lord Alfred Milner.

4. In 1903, at the bidding of Rothschild and Milner, Morgan established the American chapter of the Pilgrim Society at the Waldorf Astoria in New York. A London chapter already had been established.

J. P. Morgan
created a secret society in America to advance the goals of Cecil Rhodes.

5. The Pilgrim Society included such notables as Elihu Root, Thomas W. Lamont, Percy Rockefeller, Ogden Mills Reid, Otto Kahn, Andrew Mellon, W.B. Whitney, Cornelius Vanderbilt, Vincent Astor, Mortimer I. Schiff, Frank Vanderlip, Henry Davison, Charles D. Norton, Nelson Aldrich, and Paul Warburg.

6. The pilgrims from the London and New York societies were welcome guests at each other's clubs and shared in each other's efforts to advance a concept that they called the "New World Order."

7. The meetings of the Pilgrim Society were held in secret. No guests were allowed to attend. No minutes were kept. No financial records were disclosed.

8. Eventually, members in the Pilgrim Society came to include John Foster Dulles, Allen Dulles, General George Marshall (of the Marshall Plan), W. Averill Harriman, Joseph P. Kennedy, Henry Luce (founder of *Time* magazine), Henry Kissinger, General Alexander Haig, William Paley (CBS president), Walter Cronkite, Sandra Day O'Connor, Elliot Richardson, Jacob Schiff, Paul Volker, and David Rockefeller.

DISCUSSION

A. Discuss the relationship of the Pilgrim Societies to the Roundtable Movement.

_____

_____

_____

_____

B. What were the common characteristics of the members of the Pilgrim Societies?

_____

_____

_____

_____

C. How did the Pilgrim Society in America come to play an integral part in the formation of political policy?

_____

_____

_____

_____

D. Discuss the relationship between the House of Morgan and the House of Rothschild.

_____

_____

_____

_____

E. Why is so little known about the Pilgrim Society?

_____

_____

_____

_____

10

THE DUCK HUNTERS

1. The House of Morgan, which remained bound to the House of Rothschild, emerged as the dominant force in the creation of a deep state that would rule the United States from the shadows.

2. The origin of the Federal Reserve System dates back to the Panic of 1907, when snowballing bank runs, prompted by Morgan-generated stories about the insolvency of the Knickerbocker Trust Company, caused the collapse of banks throughout the country. Depositors were left with no means of recovering their savings; Wall Street brokers could not obtain the loans required for their daily transactions; and no central agency existed to clean up the mess.

Nelson Aldrich Rockefeller
would become the vice-president under Gerald Ford in 1974.

3. To avert another panic, Congress approved the Aldrich-Vreeland Act of 1908, which brought into being the National Monetary Commission. Senator Nelson Aldrich, who received the appointment to head the Commission, was "J.P. Morgan's floor broker in the Senate."

4. J.P. Morgan invited members of the Commission and a host of Wall Street bankers to a "duck shooting party" on Jekyll Island, off the coast of Georgia. The group included Frank A. Vanderlip, president of the National City Bank of New York (a Rockefeller firm in which Morgan was a principal shareholder); Abraham Platt Andrew, Assistant Secretary of the Treasury; Charles D. Norton, president of J.P. Morgan's First National Bank of New York; Benjamin Strong, president of J.P. Morgan's Bankers Trust Company; and Paul Warburg, one of the founders of Kuhn, Loeb and Company, a financial firm tightly connected to Rothschild.

5. The gathering was to serve the following purposes: (1) to ensure that the money trust would gain complete control over the nation's financial resources; (2) to make the money supply elastic in order to reverse the trend of private capital formation and to recapture the industrial loan market; (3) to pool the resources of the nation's banks into one reserve that would serve to protect a few of them from currency drains and bank runs; and (4) to shift inevitable financial losses from the money trust to the U.S. taxpayers.

DISCUSSION

A. Discuss the creation of the Panic of 1907.

_____

_____

_____

_____

B. Why was the creation of the Federal Reserve System crucial to the formation of the New World Order?

_____

_____

_____

_____

C. Discuss the evolution of centralized banking.

_____

_____

_____

_____

D. How does the Federal Reserve control the lives of ordinary Americans?

_____

_____

_____

_____

E. Discuss fiat money and the principles of fractional banking.

_____

_____

_____

_____

F. How did Paul Warburg emerge as one of the most powerful figures in American history?

_____

_____

_____

_____

G. How did Woodrow Wilson become a pawn of the power elite? Why did his presidency mark a turning point in American history?

_____

_____

_____

_____

AMERICA'S CENTRAL BANK

Time and time again, Americans were warned that a single overarching bank that manufactures currency would be more formidable and powerful than all the armies and navies in the world. Such advice was tossed aside on December 23, 1913, when the Federal Reserve Act became law. A cabal of international bankers now could create prosperity by flooding the banks with newly minted currency or bring about a depression by shutting down the money mills.

11

"CONTROL OF THE WORLD"

1. The money trust under J.P. Morgan "rigged" the election of 1912 to ensure the election of Woodrow Wilson, who was close to Andrew Carnegie, shared Carnegie's ideology, and became a trustee of the Carnegie Foundation.

2. On December 23, 1913, the Federal Reserve Act became law. The House vote was 298 to 60; the Senate 43 to 25.

3. The Federal Reserve began operations on November 16, 1914, with a capital base of $143,000,000. The money came from the sale of shares in the twelve district banks. The payments to the Fed's Board of Governors in Washington, D.C. arrived in the form of gold bullion. Each district bank of the Fed was a separate tax-exempt corporation with nine directors from its region's banking and

Woodrow Wilson
For the Democratic candidate, the trust opted for Woodrow Wilson, an austere, scholarly figure, who lived his life in the shadow of Wall Street.

business community. The shares, in accordance with Section 7 of the Federal Reserve Act, were all owned by private banks and individuals, who received yearly dividends in the amount of 6 percent of the net revenue.

4. The largest shareholder was the Rockefeller-controlled National City Bank, with 30,000 shares; the second largest was the Morgan-controlled First National Bank, with 15,000 shares.

5. The fact that foreign banks purchased substantial shares in the Federal Reserve System ensured that the economic course of the United States would no longer be controlled and directed solely by representatives of the American people but by a clique of very wealthy bankers from London, Paris, Hamburg, Berlin, and Rome.

6. By authorizing a central bank to control the country's money supply and the value of a dollar, Congress enabled government spending to skyrocket beyond all expectation. Politicians now could commit to projects that cost millions of dollars more than the existing revenue. The Fed, in turn, could purchase the "excess" debt by printing more paper money, thereby inflating the economy. States, seduced by the federal "deep pockets" but lacking any mechanism to manufacture debt, would become dependent on Washington, D.C. for revenue, thereby reversing the traditional relationship that existed between state and federal governments. And the taxpayers would bear the brunt of bloated governments, thanks to the enactment of a graduated income tax.

DISCUSSION

A. How did the Federal Reserve come to undermine American democracy?

_____

_____

_____

_____

B. Discuss the role of the Federal Reserve in the creation of an international money cartel.

_____

_____

_____

_____

C. How did the Federal Reserve of New York emerge as the world's most powerful bank?

_____

_____

_____

_____

D. Discuss the pivotal role of the House of Morgan in advancing the vision of Cecil Rhodes.

_____

_____

_____

_____

E. Discuss the implementation of the graduated income tax and the rise of the power elite.

_____

_____

_____

_____

F. How did it come to pass that America's wealthiest individuals came to pay little or no income tax?

_____

_____

_____

_____

G. How can the Federal Reserve be reformed or abolished?

_____

_____

_____

_____

PART THREE

WAR TO END ALL WARS

"I am concerned for the security of our great nation; not so much because of any threat from without, but because of the insidious forces working from within."
—GENERAL DOUGLAS MACARTHUR

"It is incumbent on every generation to pay its own debts as it goes. A principle which if acted on would save one-half the wars of the world."
—THOMAS JEFFERSON

"The invisible Money Power is working to control and enslave mankind. It financed Communism, Fascism, Marxism, Zionism, Socialism. All of these are directed to making the United States a member of a World Government."
—AMERICAN MERCURY MAGAZINE, DECEMBER 1957, PG. 92.

12

THE SERPENT'S EGG

1. The Houses of Carnegie and Morgan became intertwined when Carnegie became one of the co-signers of a $500 million loan from J.P. Morgan and Company to the Anglo-French Financial Commission in 1914. The $500 million to fund the Allied war against Germany represented the largest foreign loan in Wall Street history. It was five times greater than the previous record-holder, the $100 million loan to Great Britain for the Boer War. With such a tremendous amount at stake, it was essential to tip the scales in favor of the Allies by securing the participation of the United States in the conflict.

2. An incident had to be manufactured which would provoke the American people to abandon their stance of isolationism and to enter the fracas. It came with the sinking of the *Lusitania* by a German submarine on May 7, 1915.

3. After the sinking of the *Lusitania*, stories about German atrocities began to capture headlines in U.S. newspapers, including the *New York Times.* One story reported that German soldiers were deliberately mutilating Belgian babies by cutting off their hands, in some cases even eating them.

4. With the media in the control of Morgan, the American people never really knew the reason the "doughboys" were being dispatched to the trenches of France. They had been informed by leading journalists, including Roundtable member Walter Lippmann, that the cause of the war was the

assassination of Archduke Franz Ferdinand, the heir to the Austro-Hungarian Empire, by a Serbian nationalist on June 28, 1914. They were shielded from the fact that the war—like all wars—had been sparked by economic interests and that the conflict had been in the works for decades. The creation of the German empire under Bismarck upset the "balance of powers" that had existed in Europe for more than two centuries. England ruled supreme over the continent until 1871.

DISCUSSION

A. What were the economic causes of World War I?

_____

_____

_____

_____

B. How did Germany come to pose a threat to the British Empire?

_____

_____

_____

_____

C. Why did the sinking of the *Lusitania* represent a planned disaster?

_____

_____

_____

_____

D. Discuss the control of the media by the power elite and the use of propaganda to mold public opinion.

_____

_____

_____

_____

E. Explain the importance of fake news for the power elite.

_____

_____

_____

_____

F. What explains the power elite's indifference to the loss of human life and the horrors of war?

_____

_____

_____

_____

G. Could World War I have been prevented? Why? Why not?

_____

_____

_____

_____

13

MAKING HAY

1. Once America entered World War I, the Carnegie trustees under Elihu Root sent a telegram to President Woodrow Wilson, urging him not to end the war too soon.

2. Jennings C. Wise, Wilson's biographer, acknowledged that the war had been escalated and prolonged to lay the foundation for world government. He wrote: "Whether or not [British Ambassador Sir Cecil] Spring-Rice was correct in his belief that [Theodore] Marburg [the force behind the Carnegie-funded League to Enforce Peace] and the Internationalists had brought on the war, certain it is they proposed to 'make hay' out of it."

3. The war had been orchestrated from start to end not by politicians and military officials but rather by British bankers and businessmen who sought to preserve British economic hegemony. It was fueled by American financiers and industrialists who made immense profits from the bloody conflict. And it was prolonged by the efforts of the trustees of leading American foundations, including the Carnegie Endowment for International Peace, the members of which believed that the phoenix of a New World Order would emerge from the ashes of the conflagration.

4. In 1917, America's money trust, who created the Pilgrim Societies and the Roundtable, funded the Russian Revolution with the conviction not only that it would spark a universal movement for global government, but also that the revolution would permit them to give control of Russia's vast natural resources.

5. After the Bolsheviks seized power, Standard Oil, under the direction of the House of Rockefeller, purchased the Russian oil fields, set up a refinery for the Soviets, and made arrangements to market the refined oil in Europe. During the 1920s, the Rockefellers' Chase Bank set up the American-Russian Chamber of Commerce, financed the raw material exports of the Soviets, and sold Russian bonds to American investors.

6. The war gave rise to modern warfare. Huge plants sprouted up throughout the United States to produce military aircraft, submarines, battleships, aircraft carriers, tanks, portable machine guns, flamethrowers, and automatic rifles. Military spending rose until it constituted 22 percent of the GNP in 1918. The principal beneficiaries were U.S. Steel, Bethlehem Steel, DuPont Chemical, Kennecott, and General Electric—all of which were related to the House of Morgan.

DISCUSSION

A. List the reasons why the power elite sought to prolong World War I?

B. Why did the planners of the New World Order support the rise of international communism?

C. Why is big government integral to the needs of the power elite?

_____

_____

_____

_____

D. How did World War I give rise to the formation of the military-industrial complex?

_____

_____

_____

_____

E. How did the House of Morgan and the House of Rockefeller profit from World War I?

_____

_____

_____

_____

F. Why was World War I necessary for the establishment of big government?

_____

_____

_____

_____

THE PRODUCTION OF FALSE NEWS.

World War I was produced by the perpetuation of fake news. The babies in Belgium were not mutilated and Catholic nuns did not have their breasts hacked off by barbaric Huns, and the *Lusitania* was sunk when the British High Command lured the ship to a site where a German U-boat was waiting. Millions were sent to their deaths because they believed what they read in the newspapers.

14

PEACE AND PUNISHMENT

1. By the Treaty of Versailles, which was signed on July 28, 1919, Germany lost one-tenth of her population and one-eighth of her territory. Germany's overseas empire, the third largest in the world, was torn apart and handed over to the victors. German citizens who lived in these German colonies were obliged to forfeit all of their personal property. Japan was given the German concession in Shantung and the German islands north of the equator. The German islands south of the equator were handed over to Australia and New Zealand. Germany's African colonies were shelled out to Britain, South Africa, and France. Germany was also required to cede to the Allies the city of Danzig and its hinterlands, including the delta of the Vistula River on the Baltic Sea. This last stipulation would spark World War II, since the Germans, residing in Danzig, would call upon Adolf Hitler to liberate them from the clutches of the League of Nations.

2. The loss of empire was only a part of the punishment. Germany was forbidden to build armored cars and tanks, to produce heavy artillery, and to maintain an air force. Her High Seas Fleet and merchant ships were confiscated as booty. And the German army was restricted to a force of 100,000 men. And then there was the matter of finances. Germany was required not only to pay the pensions of the Allied soldiers but also to cough up thirty-two billion gold marks—an amount equivalent to the entire wealth of the country—in reparations. This indemnity would be used to repay, with interest, the loans the international bankers had provided to Great Britain and France.

3. The German diplomats agreed to these terms because the Allied forces, including U.S. warships, had imposed a blockade on Germany, sealing all points of entry so that food, medical supplies and other vital necessities could not flow into the country. The "starvation" blockade, which persisted from November 11, 1918 through the peace conference, was responsible for the deaths of 900,000 men, women, and children, all after the Germans had laid down their arms.

4. The trustees of the Carnegie Endowment for International Peace took an active role in the Paris Peace Conference and the creation of the League of Nations. James T. Shotwell, CEIP's director of research, accompanied Wilson to the Conference, along with Colonel House, Charles Haskins, a trustee of the Carnegie Corporation, and CEIP trustee John W. Foster's grandsons John Foster and Allen Dulles. Equally prominent among the entourage was Thomas W. Lamont, Morgan's leading partner, whose mission was to ensure that Britain and France would repay the enormous loans they had received from the House of Morgan, and Paul Warburg, the chairman of the Federal Reserve, who represented America's banking interests.

5. One of the planks of the Versailles Treaty called for severe reparations to be paid to the victorious nations by the German government, including the pensions of the Allied soldiers. This stipulation precipitated the "hyperinflation" of the German mark between 1920 and 1923, the destruction of the German middle class in Germany, and the rise of the Third Reich. It had been written and inserted into the peace settlement by John Foster Dulles, one of the founders of the Council on Foreign Relations, and Thomas Lamont, J.P. Morgan's business partner.

6. As an addendum to the Treaty of Versailles, the victorious nations drafted the Charter of the League of Nations, which was signed by President Wilson on behalf of the American government.

7. By the time Wilson set sail for his return trip to America, the dream of Cecil Rhodes was on the threshold of becoming a reality. His secret society of aristocratic and mostly effete Masons had gained control of the Empire and reshaped the world. German islands in the South Pacific had been handed over to Australia and New Zealand. Mesopotamia and Palestine, taken from the Ottoman Empire, had been granted to Britain. German South West Africa became incorporated into South Africa, which remained under British rule. The Cameroons and Togoland were divided between Britain and France. Thanks to "the war to end all wars," the British Empire had gained 950,000 square miles and millions of new subjects.

8. Only one part of the grand scheme remained to be set in place: the reunification of Britain and the United States. This task could be easily accomplished through the League of Nations, since Britain would wield political and economic control over almost every member nation. A reunification, Lionel Curtis wrote in *The Commonwealth of Nations*, would allow America to advance beyond the concept of nationalism and to accept its obligation to join with Great Britain in an effort to impose peace, order, and good government over the "backward nations." Americans, he believed, were ready for this undertaking since "the presence of the Negro in their midst has taught them that a mixture in one country of an advanced with a backward civilization is in itself the greatest menace to liberty."

9. When Wilson submitted the treaty for ratification in June of 1919, the Senate balked. The establishment of the League, Senator Henry Cabot Lodge maintained, would make Wilson "the president of the world." The setback was so personally devastating for Wilson that he suffered a severe stroke in October of 1919 that prevented him from seeking a third term in office.

DISCUSSION

A. How did the Treaty of Versailles transform the world order?

_____

_____

_____

_____

B. Discuss the participation of the United States in the starvation blockade against the German people.

_____

_____

_____

_____

C. Outline the reasons why the Treaty of Versailles gave rise to World War II.

_____

_____

_____

_____

D. Discuss the impact of World War I and the Treaty of Versailles on the British Empire.

_____

_____

_____

_____

E. What was the ultimate goal of the League of Nations?

_____

_____

_____

_____

F. Why was the League rejected by the U.S. Senate?

_____

_____

_____

_____

PART FOUR

THE AMERICAN ESTABLISHMENT

"I predict future happiness for Americans if they can prevent the government from wasting the labors of the people under the pretense of taking care of them."
—THOMAS JEFFERSON

"We are grateful to the Washington Post, the New York Times, Time magazine and other great publications whose directors have attended our meetings and respected the promises of discretion for almost forty years. It would have been impossible for us to develop our plan for the world if we had been subject to the bright lights of publicity during those years. But, the world is now more sophisticated and prepared to march towards a world-government. The supranational sovereignty of an intellectual elite and world bankers is surely preferable to the national auto determination practiced in past centuries."
—DAVID ROCKEFELLER IN AN ADDRESS TO A TRILATERAL COMMISSION MEETING IN

JUNE OF 1991

15

THE SHADOW GOVERNMENT

1. On May 30, 1919, members of the American and British delegations, all of whom were members of the Roundtable movement, met at the Majestic Hotel in Paris to create the Institute for International Affairs, which was to have two chapters: the Royal Institute of International Affairs (RIIA, also known as the Chatham House Study Group) as an advisory group to the British Government, and the Council on Foreign Relations as a "think tank" for the U.S. State Department.

Council on Foreign Relations
The Council on Foreign Relations (CFR) became a place where enterprising bankers and businessmen gathered to gain access to America's power elite.

A subsidiary organization, the Institute of Pacific Relations, was formed to deal exclusively with Far Eastern Affairs. Other organizations were set up in Paris and Hamburg.

2. The House of Morgan spearheaded the formation of the Council on Foreign Relations (CFR) on July 29, 1921. John W. Davis, the first president of the organization, was one of Morgan's private attorneys.

3. In post-World War I America, Morgan and Company wielded almost unlimited power. Its financial resources defied statistical measurement, since the full extent of its control over American banks and businesses remained concealed from public scrutiny. Ten years after the formation of the CFR Ferdinand Lindberg was able to list 80 financial institutions and 86 non-financial corporations under the Morgan influence. These firms possessed combined assets of $77,600,000,000, a total that represented more than one-fourth of America's corporate wealth.

4. The Morgan amount did not include the holdings of the House of Rockefeller, which had become intertwined with Morgan interests through their financial and industrial alliance. By the turn of the 20th century, this alliance had become so close that it was difficult for financial analysts to discern what holdings belonged to Morgan and what belonged to Rockefeller.

5. Through the years, the Council on Foreign Relations remained under the domain of the Houses of Morgan, Rothschild, and, eventually, Rockefeller. These banking families controlled it. They financed it. They selected its staff. They set its agenda. They arranged the placement of its members in key government positions. Its purpose was to align America's foreign policy with the aim of the international money cartel, in the same manner that the Federal Reserve aligned America's economic policy. Its activities were never benign and never removed from the ultimate goal of its founders: the accumulation of the world's wealth.

6. The corporate membership list of the Council on Foreign Relations contains the names of almost every major business and bank in the country, including Bank of America, Merrill Lynch, Chevron, ExxonMobil, JPMorgan Chase, Morgan Stanley, Goldman Sachs, Shell Oil, American Express, Barclays, Lockheed Martin, Lazard, Soros Fund Management, Prudential Financial, IBM, General Electric, Facebook, FedEx, Rothschild North America, Northrop Grumman, Microsoft, Raytheon, Merck and Company, Standard and Poor's, Sony Corporation of America, Time Warner, and Walmart. A small sampling of the prominent names on the 2015 membership roster

is as follows: Elliot Abrams, Madeleine Albright, Bruce Babbitt, James Baker, Warren Beatty, Michael Bloomberg, Sidney Blumenthal, John Bolton, Zbigniew Brzezinski, Warren Buffet, Paul Bremer, Jimmy Carter, Dick Cheney, Warren Christopher, Henry Cisneros, Wesley Clark, Bill Clinton, Chelsea Clinton, George Clooney, Katie Couric, Scott Cuomo, Christopher Dodd, Alfonse D'Amato, Diane Feinstein, Timothy Geithner, Ruth Bader Ginsburg, Alan Greenspan, Chuck Hagel, Teresa Kerry Heinz, Vernon Jordan, Joseph Kennedy III, Edward Kennedy, Jr., Henry Kissinger, Charles Krauthammer, John Kerry, Bernard Lewis, Joe Lieberman, John McCain, George Mitchell, Janet Negroponte, Alice Rivlin, Grover Norquist, Sam Nunn, Janet Napolitano, Colin Powell, Condoleezza Rice, John Roberts, John D. Rockefeller IV, David Rockefeller, David Rockefeller Jr., Nicholas Rockefeller, Steven Rockefeller, Donna Shalala, Susan Rice, Douglas Schoen, Joe Scarborough, William Roper, George Soros, Jonathan Soros, Lesley Stahl, Diane Sawyer, Laura Tyson, Cyrus Vance, Barbara Walters, Paul Wolfowitz, and Janet Yellen.

7. In 1957, a Congressional investigative committee revealed that the Council on Foreign Relations clandestinely serves to promote "internationalism" in a particular sense—a form directed toward "world government" and to create derogation of American "nationalism."

8. In keeping with the founding spirit of the Council on Foreign Relations, John Dewey, noted educator and philosopher, co-authored *The Humanist Manifesto*, which called for a "synthesis of all religions" and a "socialized and cooperative economic order." Similarly, social engineer Lewis Mumford and theologian Reinhold Niebuhr, two *Foreign Affairs* correspondents, wrote in their work *The City of Man: A Declaration of World Democracy*: "Universal peace can be founded only by the unity of man under one law and one government … All states, deflated and disciplined, must align themselves under the law of the world-state … the new order … when the heresy of nationalism is conquered and the absurd architecture of the present world is finally dismantled. … And there must be a common creed … or ethico-religious purpose."

9. Within the hallowed halls of the Council on Foreign Relations, a carefully selected group of candidates are groomed for prominent positions of power in the federal government. "They walk in one door as acquisitive businessmen," David Halberstam said, "and come out the other as statesmen-figures."

10. The CFR holds 120 meetings a year at the Pratt House in New York City. These meetings are held in secrecy under the rule of "non-attribution," which means that everything that transpires at the meetings is off the record. Anyone who violates this rule which prohibits statements from members reaching the press is subject to immediate expulsion from the organization.

11. The council also sponsors a yearly average of twenty study groups that concentrate on specific foreign policy topics. These groups produce reports that are circulated among an inner core of members. The preparation of these reports do not represent idle academic exercises, but rather the means to advance the agenda of the CFR inner core. Admiral Chester Ward, another former council member, wrote: "Once the ruling members of the CFR have decided that the U.S. Government should adopt a particular policy, the very substantial research facilities of CFR are put to work to develop arguments, intellectual and emotional, to support the new policy, and to confound and discredit, intellectually and politically, any opposition." Indeed, the studies generated by the Council have resulted in the establishment of such international institutions as the United Nations, the World Bank, and the International Monetary Fund.

12. Proof of the power of the CFR resides in the fact that by 2017, twenty Secretaries of State, nineteen Secretaries of the Treasury, fifteen Secretaries of Defense, and hundreds of other federal department heads have been CFR members, along with twenty-one of the twenty-four CIA Directors, and every chairman of the Federal Reserve since 1951.

13. Financing for the study groups comes from the Rockefeller, Carnegie, and Ford foundations, which are governed by boards of directors that are interconnected.

DISCUSSION

A. How did the CFR complement the operation of the Federal Reserve?

_____

_____

_____

_____

B. Discuss the importance of the Chatham House Rule to the workings of the CFR.

_____

_____

_____

_____

C. Discuss the means by which the interests of the various banking families became intertwined within the CFR.

_____

_____

_____

_____

D. Why is the CFR a subversive organization?

_____

_____

_____

_____

E. How are members of the CFR recruited?

_____

_____

_____

_____

F. Discuss the workings of the CFR study groups and the means by which these groups have established American political policy.

_____

_____

_____

_____

G. Explain the means by which the CFR is controlled by the House of Rockefeller.

_____

_____

_____

_____

CIRCLES WITHIN CIRCLES

The Council on Foreign Relations has been structured with circles within circles, in keeping with Cecil Rhodes and his Society of the Elect. At its core were members of the House of Morgan and the House of Rockefeller who drafted national and international policy in conjunction with the Royal Institute of International Affairs and the House of Rothschild.

16

A DESIGNED DEPRESSION

1. In the wake of World War I, America became the world's largest creditor nation. The money that flowed into America from the $8 billion in war loans granted to France, Great Britain, and Italy was used to fund U.S. business and industry and to provide loans to American workers.

2. While Europe remained in a state of stagnancy, perpetuated by the devastation of property and loss of population caused by the war, cars, highways, bridges, manufacturing plants, hotels, theaters and department stores were being built throughout America at an unprecedented rate. Unemployment dropped to less than 5 percent. Almost every home in the country had electricity. By 1920, the national income of the United States was greater than the combined incomes of Britain, France, Germany, Japan, Canada, and seventeen smaller countries.

3. The Morgans and the Rockefellers controlled not only America's leading national banks but also the Federal Reserve System. By the snap of their fingers, these banking families, since they had provided the funding that produced the country's prosperity and controlled the cash flow, could alter the course of the American economy, plunging the American people into the depths of poverty.

4. The Depression was created so that the American people would become more docile and more easily governed through the strong arm of government, applied by a central power of wealth under leading financiers.

5. It was implemented by a process known as the "24-hour call." This process enabled investors to purchase securities on extended credit. This meant if a person wanted to purchase $1,000 in stock, he only had to shell out $100. The loan was immediate, and it was provided by every national bank in the country.

6. The loans, which had been given with a mere ten percent down, could be recalled at a moment's notice, forcing the borrowers to come up a full repayment within twenty-four hours. For most Americans, the only way to make repayments was by selling all of their securities. The stage was set for the crisis.

7. On February 6, 1929, Montagu Norman arrived in Washington to confer with Treasury Secretary Andrew Mellon. Immediately after the mysterious meeting, the Federal Reserve Board began to cut the money supply and to raise the interest rate.

8. On "Black Friday," October 24, 1929, the excrement hit the fan. Throughout the country, the loans were called and the stampede to sell stocks began. The stock market crashed; banks throughout the country ran out of cash and closed up shop; and the Fed refused to come to the rescue with a printing of fresh currency.

9. The crash may have devastated the average American investor but not "Junior" Rockefeller, "Jack" Morgan, Bernard Baruch, Joseph P. Kennedy, Paul Warburg and other financial insiders. They were either out of the market or had sold "short" so that they earned enormous profits as the Dow Jones plummeted. Following the crash, they swooped down on Wall Street like vultures to feast on ravaged companies. Shares that once sold for a dollar now could be bought for a few pennies.

DISCUSSION

A. Discuss the emergence of the United States as the leading world power at the close of World War I.

_____

_____

_____

_____

B. How did the Morgan and Rockefeller families profit from the Dawes Plan?

_____

_____

_____

_____

C. Discuss the way in which the Dawes Plan gave birth to the Third Reich.

_____

_____

_____

_____

D. How did the implementation of the "24-hour call" cause the stock market crash?

_____

_____

_____

_____

E. Explain how the Federal Reserve could have prevented the Wall Street Massacre.

_____

_____

_____

_____

F. How did the power elite benefit from the crash?

_____

_____

_____

_____

G. What was the ultimate purpose of the "designed" Depression?

_____

_____

_____

_____

17

THE POLICE STATE

1. By 1932, unemployment stood at 25 percent. The Gross National Product had slipped to 50 percent. Farmers had lost 60 percent of their income. Twenty percent of the country's banks had gone belly-up. Breadlines had formed in every town and city throughout the country.

2. On June 6, 1933, Congress ratified the National Industrial Recovery Act (NIRA), which represented the heart of the New Deal.

3. Every industry was to operate in collaboration with the federal government in setting prices, wages, quantities of product, and working conditions. Under this system, the companies with the most employees had the most clout in determining policy.

4. In the iron and steel industry, Morgan's U.S. Steel possessed 511 votes, Allegheny Steel, 17 votes, and Bethlehem Steel, 16 votes. Giant corporations now possessed the ability to impose production, salary, and price standards that would drive their competition out of business.

5. Monopolies were now supported and sustained by federal mandate. Regulations ran amuck. The agency approved 557 basic and 189 supplemental industry codes in two years. Between 4,000 and 5,000 business practices were prohibited, some 3,000 administrative orders were promulgated in documents of over 10,000 pages, and tens of thousands of legal opinions were upheld and enforced by NIRA officials.

6. To enforce the regulations, the NIRA employed its own police force.

7. On May 27, 1935, the Supreme Court ruled that the NIRA violated the borders of the U.S. Constitution.

8. The New Deal represented more than an attempt to impose a fascist system of government upon the American people. It also constituted a concerted attempt by the House of Rockefeller to gain control of the Federal Reserve and financial domination of the United States.

9. The harbinger of this revolution was the Rockefeller's successful takeover of the Morgan's flagship commercial bank, Chase National Bank of New York.

DISCUSSION

A. How did the National Industrial Recovery Act (NIRA) undermine American democracy?

_____

_____

_____

_____

B. How did the NIRA serve the interests of the power elite?

_____

_____

_____

_____

C. Why are regulations integral to sustain big business?

_____

_____

_____

_____

D. Why did the Supreme Court rule that the NIRA was unconstitutional?

_____

_____

_____

_____

E. Explain the significance of the merger of the Chase National Bank of New York with the Equitable Trust Company.

_____

_____

_____

_____

PART FIVE

THE OCCULT ECONOMY

"No free man shall ever be debarred the use of arms."
—THOMAS JEFFERSON

"[The New World Order] cannot happen without US participation, as we are the most significant single component. Yes, there will be a New World Order, and it will force the United States to change its perceptions."
—HENRY KISSINGER, WORLD AFFAIRS COUNCIL PRESS CONFERENCE, REGENT BEVERLY WILSHIRE HOTEL, APRIL 19, 1994.

"To compel a man to subsidize with his taxes the propagation of ideas which he disbelieves and abhors is sinful and tyrannical."
—THOMAS JEFFERSON

18

CONFISCATED GOLD

1. For centuries, the banking system was based on a gold standard, and the price of gold was established by law. In the United States, this price, prior to the arrival of FDR in the White House, was fixed at $20.07 per ounce.

2. This set price served not only to prevent inflation and deflation but also to establish the limits of the money supply since honest paper currency could not be issued without adequate principal—that is, gold.

3. When Roosevelt became president, the United States had the largest gold reserves of any nation in the world.

Franklin D. Roosevelt
In 1933, when Roosevelt became president, the United States had the largest gold reserves of any nation in the world. On April 5, 1933, Roosevelt responded to the mounting banking crisis by ordering all American citizens to surrender their gold to the government.

4. On April 5, 1933, Roosevelt ordered all American citizens to surrender their gold to the government. No one in America was allowed to own more than $100 in gold coins.

5. The federal mandate implied that government was the rightful owner of all the gold in the nation and that no American had a right to possess the precious metal.

6. The confiscated gold was turned over to the Federal Reserve.

7. The Fed began to churn out cash at an unprecedented level.

8. The dollar lost 93 percent of its purchasing power, while the value of an ounce of gold rose to $35.

9. Under the direction of the Council on Foreign Relations, Roosevelt secretly removed America from the gold standard. Informed of this decision, Lewis Douglas, the Director of the Bureau of the Budget, proclaimed "the end of Western Civilization."

10. As the Depression deepened, the Federal Reserve began to purchase the foreign debts of Germany, France, and Great Britain to provide steamer trunks filled with bonds and notes to prop up failing foreign economies, while so much gold continued to pour into the vaults of the Federal Reserve in New York that Roosevelt ordered the creation of Fort Knox, another federal gold depository, in Louisville, Kentucky.

DISCUSSION

A. What was the importance of the gold standard?

_____

_____

_____

_____

B. Why did Franklin D. Roosevelt order the confiscation of the gold owned and held by the American citizens?

_____

_____

_____

_____

C. What accounts for the failure of the American people to rise in protest against the government's confiscation of their wealth?

_____

_____

_____

_____

D. How did the Federal Reserve make use of the gold to further its objection of creating a one-world economy?

_____

_____

_____

_____

E. What happened to Fort Knox?

_____

_____

_____

_____

19

THE MOTHER BANK

1. On May 17, 1930, during the Great Depression, the Bank for International Settlements (BIS), a private financial institution, opened its headquarters in Basel, Switzerland.

2. The major shareholders were the Bank of England, the Bank of France, the National Bank of Belgium, Reichsbank, the J.P. Morgan Company, the Morgan-owned First National Bank of New York, the Morgan-owned First National Bank of Chicago, and the Bank of Japan.

3. Eventually, the Federal Reserve would purchase shares in the Basel bank and become the leading player in directing its activities.

BIS
On May 17, 1930, during the Great Depression, the Bank of International Settlements (BIS), a private financial institution, opened its headquarters in Basel, Switzerland.

4. The original purpose of the BIS was to facilitate the recurring problem of the war reparations that had been imposed upon Germany.

5. But the BIS, in its statement of purpose, made no mention of the mandated reparations. It rather maintained that its objective was "to promote the cooperation of central banks and to provide additional facilities for international operations; and to act as trustees or agents in regard to international financial settlements entrusted to it under agreements with the parties concerned." Throughout its history, the BIS referred to itself not as an institution of settlements, but rather as "the central banker's central bank," a place where bankers could meet in secret away from the prying eyes of the press and the nagging demands of the politicians.

6. Meetings of the BIS shareholders were held under tight security and complete secrecy. No minutes, agenda, or attendance list was published in any form, and the building became "inviolate," meaning that the Swiss authorities possessed no authority over its premises. Correspondence to the bank was received by diplomatic couriers.

7. As soon as it was established, the BIS took up the task of stabilizing the world's economies by allocating control of the gold reserves that were held by its member banks.

8. Gold now flowed out of China, Japan, Europe, and the United States into Basel.

9. Thanks to the power of this combined wealth, the BIS could save a country from economic disaster or drive it into a tailspin. And its transnational actions could take place without political or governmental interference.

10. By manipulating the money supply and determining the value of all currencies, the directors of the BIS could hold absolute control over state and society.

DISCUSSION

A. What was the stated purpose of the Bank for International Settlements (BIS)?

_____

_____

_____

_____

B. Who were the major shareholders?

_____

_____

_____

_____

C. What was the clandestine purpose of the BIS?

_____

_____

_____

_____

D. Why were the meetings of BIS shareholders held under utmost security and complete secrecy?

_____

_____

_____

_____

E. Discuss the difference between capital and money.

_____

_____

_____

_____

F. How did the BIS exercise control over international affairs?

_____

_____

_____

_____

THE FLOW OF GOLD

The confiscation of gold from the American people by the Roosevelt Administration and the transfer of this gold to the Bank for International Settlements in Basel is one of the pivotal developments in modern history. And yet this event receives scant attention in college courses of economics or political science.

20

THE MOTHER BOXES

1. The secret shipments of gold to Basel allowed the Federal Reserve and the Bank for International Settlements to create an occult economy.

2. In exchange for the precious metal received for "safekeeping," bonds and notes of astronomical value were issued by the Fed and dispatched to the BIS, which deployed them to central and commercial banks throughout the world to bolster flailing economies.

3. The worth of the bonds and notes was based on the value of the gold that had been "black-listed," i.e., removed from the market and stored away in vaults from circulation and scrutiny.

"This box is officially declared sealed and registered by the Department of Treasury on April 22, 1934, Washington, D.C. U.S.A., complete with contents of important bank documents; a lawful instrument for redemption engagement and other commercial purposes."

4. If the public discovered how much precious metal actually existed in storage, economic shock waves would reverberate throughout the world, and gold would lose much of its value overnight.

5. On the eve of the Sino-Japanese War, wealthy Chinese families delivered their gold reserves to Chiang Kai-Shek, the leader of Nationalist China, for safekeeping in the Federal Reserve.

6. In exchange for these deposits, the Chinese families received guarantees from the Fed in the form of billion-dollar bonds.

7. This extraordinary deployment of gold certificates from the Federal Reserve served to establish the dollar as the currency for international exchange and to fortify the United States as the economic bedrock of a world ravaged by war and depression.

8. The bonds, boxes, and chests contained deliberate, glaring errors in spelling and grammar so that they would be dismissed as fake by almost any public official or banking authority who examined them.

DISCUSSION

A. Why were the Mother Boxes created?

_____

_____

_____

_____

B. What accounts for the astronomical worth of the bonds and notes within the boxes?

_____

_____

_____

_____

C. Why was the existence of the Mother Boxes concealed from the public?

_____

_____

_____

_____

D. Why was the "Treaty of Versailles" engraved on the boxes?

_____

_____

_____

_____

E. Why were the bonds, notes, and chests engraved with glaring errors?

_____

_____

_____

_____

F. What is the purpose of the occult economy?

_____

_____

_____

_____

PART SIX

THE BREAKING OF NATIONS

"I believe that if the people of this nation fully understood what Congress has done to them over the last forty-nine years, they would move on Washington; they would not wait for an election ... It adds up to a preconceived plan to destroy the economic and social independence of the United States!"

—GEORGE W. MALONE, U.S. SENATOR (NEVADA), SPEAKING BEFORE CONGRESS IN 1957.

"The strongest reason for the people to retain the right to keep and bear arms is, as a last resort, to protect themselves against tyranny in government."

—THOMAS JEFFERSON

Winston Churchill said this back in 1920: "From the days of Spartacus-Weishaupt to those of Karl Marx, to those of Trotsky, Bela Kun, Rosa Luxembourg, and Emma Goldman, this worldwide conspiracy for the overthrow of civilization and for the reconstitution of society on the basis of arrested development, of envious malevolence and impossible equality, has been steadily growing. It played a definitely recognizable role in the tragedy of the French Revolution. It has been the mainspring of every subversive movement during the nineteenth century, and now at last this band of extraordinary personalities from the underworld of the great cities of Europe and America have gripped the Russian people by the hair of their heads, and have become practically the undisputed masters of that enormous empire."

MIDTERM REFLECTION: The plot of the Killing of Uncle Sam is linear. Cecil John Rhodes established the Society of the Elect, which, in turn, spawned the Roundtable Movement that spread throughout the British Empire. The movement crystallized into the Pilgrim Societies in London and New York. The members of these societies remained men of wealth and power who sought to break down the borders between nations, including tariffs on trade, in order to bring forth a New World Order. All of these individuals maintained a close relationship with the House of Rothschild. The leading figures in America who spearheaded this effort were Andrew Carnegie, J.P. Morgan, and John D. Rockefeller. Their first victory was the establishment of the Federal Reserve System which enslaved all American citizens to the money cartel. Their second victory came with the perpetuation of fake news and acts of terror that brought the United States into World War I. The third victory was the creation of the Council on Foreign Relations, which eventually gained control of the U.S. State Department and the ability to chart the course of American history. The ultimate goals of Rhodes and his disciples were the acquisition of the world's wealth, i.e., its natural resources, and the establishment of universal socialism.

21

THE PROBLEM WITH HITLER

1. On September 1, 1939, Hitler invaded Poland and initiated World War II. This act of alleged "unprovoked aggression" violated a "war guarantee" that British Prime Minister Neville Chamberlain had given to a junta of Polish colonels.

2. The guarantee, which was issued several months before the invasion, proclaimed that Britain would deploy all of its military power to protect Polish independence.

Adolf Hitler
Within his death camps, Hitler stands accused of exterminating over 6 million Jews, Gypsies, and people with physical disabilities.

3. Why Chamberlain offered such a guarantee remains quizzical. Britain possessed no vital interest in Poland or Eastern Europe and had drafted no plan to ward off the *Wehrmacht* (Germany army).

4. The Nazi invasion had not been unprovoked. It had been caused by the Treaty of Versailles, which stripped Germany of its territorial holdings, including the port city of Danzig—which was handed over to Poland. The population of Danzig at the time of the invasion was 97 percent German.

They turned in desperation to the Fuhrer for reunion with their countrymen. They had been subjected to ongoing attacks of wanton savagery. More than 58,000 ethnic Germans were murdered by the ruling Polish junta.

5. Throughout the war, Hitler made at least twenty-eight attempts to establish unconditional peace with Britain. They were all refused.

6. Hitler was not intent upon world conquest. His dreams of conquest remained fixed not on the West but the East and, most particularly, Russia.

7. A primary reason for the outbreak of World War II was financial. On January 7, 1939, Hjalmar Schacht, the president of the Reichsbank (German's central bank), which remained bound to the House of Rothschild and the money cartel, refused to provide a loan of three billion *Reichsmarks* to the German government.

8. Hitler responded to Schacht's demands by ousting him from office and by making the Reichsbank "totally subordinate" to the "sovereignty of the state." By transforming the central bank into a national bank, Hitler could produce paper money that he could loan without interest to the Nazi government and its citizens.

9. Within two weeks of the outbreak of war in Europe, Walter Mallory, the executive director of the CFR, and Hamilton Fish, the editor of the CFR's periodical *Foreign Affairs,* met in Washington with Assistant Secretary of State George Messersmith, another CFR member, to set up a study group which could develop a wartime strategy for the United States. The group, which met in secret, became known as the War and Peace Studies Project.

10. One of the tasks of the War and Peace Studies Project was to develop propaganda that would cause the American people to shed their isolationism and to support participation in the European war "to make the world safe for democracy."

11. Another task was to lay the groundwork for a new system of global government to replace the ill-fated League of Nations. This system would become the United Nations.

DISCUSSION

A. Why did Britain declare war on Germany in 1939?

_____

_____

_____

_____

B. Why did Hitler invade Poland?

_____

_____

_____

_____

C. What was Hitler's ultimate goal?

_____

_____

_____

_____

D. Who was Hjalmar Schacht? How did he trigger World War II?

_____

_____

_____

_____

E. Describe the economic conditions in Germany from 1933 to 1939.

_____

_____

_____

_____

F. What was the decisive proof that Hitler was not contemplating a world war?

_____

_____

_____

_____

G. Why were war plans developed by a CFR study group two years before the attack on Pearl Harbor?

_____

_____

_____

_____

22

BAITING NAZIS AND "NIPS"

1. There was much for the money cartel to gain from a second global war. War broke down borders, caused mass migrations, and gave rise to new countries. It promulgated diversity and undermined the racial structures of existing nations. This benefit of war was essential for the creation of a global government.

2. Since economic hegemony was at stake, it was essential to bring the United States into the European conflict. This task was formidable since America possessed no vital interest in the European war and the American people remained isolationists, who opted to remain free from all foreign entanglements.

3. An incident had to be staged that was even more horrific than the sinking of the *Lusitania*. Thus, the provocation began.

4. At the instigation of the Century Group and the War and Peace Studies Project, both CFR organizations, FDR shipped fifty destroyers to Great Britain to beef up the British fleet. He also sent millions of rounds of ammunition to England on freighters that sailed directly into the war zone. To add to the antagonism, FDR ordered the closing of all German consulates so that German officials would have no means of protesting the ongoing aid to Britain. In a final attempt to instigate a German attack, Roosevelt ordered the occupation of Iceland and used this strategic location to deploy depth-charges against German U-boats.

5. To bring the nation into the European conflict, Franklin Delano Roosevelt produced a bogus map to show that Hitler's design was to place South and North America under the dominion of the Third Reich. The map was a forgery drafted by William Stephenson and other British agents in New York who were operating under orders from Prime Minister Winston Churchill.

6. Roosevelt also falsely claimed that he possessed another document which showed that Hitler sought to abolish Christianity in order to produce an international Nazi church.

7. Finally, in his address to the nation, Roosevelt maintained that two German submarines had launched attacks on U.S. destroyers Greer and Kearny, the latter of which had been torpedoed, resulting in a loss of 11 American lives. "We have wished to avoid shooting," the president said. "But the shooting has started. And history has recorded who fired the first shot." The truth was the two destroyers had been tracking German subs for British planes by dropping depth charges.

8. Since Hitler refused to respond to provocation, the Century Group and the War and Peace Studies Project, under the guidance of the House of Rockefeller, looked to Japan to mount an attack against the United States. The choice was prudent since Japan, on September 27, 1940, had signed the Tripartite Pact with Germany and Italy, which bound the three nations to unite in times of war.

9. The matter of positioning the Japanese to take the first shot was taken up by the War and Peace Studies Group, which recommended the imposition of a crippling trade embargo on Japan. In July 1941, FDR imposed a trade embargo of oil, rubber, scrap metal, and steel to Japan. The reason for this action, Roosevelt explained, was Japan's occupation of French Indo-China. No one questioned this action even though the French had permitted the occupation.

10. The British government and the Dutch government in exile followed suit by placing their own oil embargos on Japan. As a result, Japan lost access to three-fourths of its overseas trade and 88 percent of its imported oil.

11. More sanctions followed. FDR froze all of Japan's financial assets in the United States and closed the Panama Canal to Japanese shipping.

12. By the fall of 1941, U.S. military intelligence had broken the radio code that Tokyo used to communicate with its embassies. The decoded intercepts made the U.S. War Department aware that Japanese spies in Hawaii were informing Tokyo of the locations of American warships docked in Pearl Harbor and the suggested date of Sunday, December 7th, for an attack.

13. This information was passed on to President Roosevelt, Secretary Stimson, and General George Marshall, the Army Chief of Staff. By December 6th, the War Department was aware that Japanese aircraft carriers had moved within 400 miles of Honolulu.

14. Despite their awareness that an attack was imminent, neither FDR nor his War Department issued an alert to Admiral Husband Kimmel and General Walter C. Short, the leading U.S. military commanders in Hawaii.

15. The attack left two thousand Americans dead and eighteen naval vessels sunk or heavily damaged.

DISCUSSION

A. Why was war essential for the creation of a global government?

_____

_____

_____

_____

B. Discuss the attempts by FDR to instigate a Nazi attack against the United States.

_____

_____

_____

_____

C. Discuss FDR's secret maps and his attempts to lure the American people into the war in Europe.

_____

_____

_____

_____

D. Discuss the "attacks" on the U.S. destroyers Greer and Kearny. How do these attacks reflect the sinking of the *Lusitania*?

_____

_____

_____

_____

E. How did the Roosevelt Administration probe Japan into launching the attack on Pearl Harbor?

_____

_____

_____

_____

F. Discuss FDR's contribution to the demise of Uncle Sam.

_____

_____

_____

_____

NO CONCERN FOR HUMANITY

World War II did not arise out of any concern over genocide or acts of Nazi barbarity. Hitler was a maniacal despot who sent millions of innocent civilians to death camps. But Stalin, who became America's ally in the war, was an equally horrific tyrant. By the time Churchill signed the Anglo-Soviet agreement on July 13, 1941, Stalin had killed 22 million, a thousand times the number of deaths attributed to Hitler. Within his death camps, Hitler stands accused of exterminating over 6 million Jews, Gypsies, and people with physical disabilities. Stalin killed 40,000 people a week, even during peacetime, for a total of 60 million.

23

THE SECRET ARMY

1. On June 13, 1941, the Office of Strategic Services (OSS), America's first intelligence agency, was set up in Rockefeller Center to "collect and analyze all information and data which may bear upon national security."

2. The agents were not ordinary men with ordinary means. Almost to a man, they were bankers, lawyers, businessmen and accountants deeply embedded with the Council on Foreign Relations and the international money cartel.

3. Allen Dulles was a prime example of an OSS agent. A scion of the Eastern Establishment, he came from a distinguished family of political dignitaries. John W. Foster, his maternal grandfather, had served as Secretary of State under Benjamin Harrison, and Robert Lansing, his uncle by marriage, had been Woodrow Wilson's Secretary of State. Dulles had attended the Paris Peace Conference with Wilson, where he had been instrumental in the creation of the Royal Institute on International Affairs and the Council on Foreign Relations.

4. Dulles was placed in charge of the OSS office in Bern, Switzerland, where he decided that America was waging a war against the wrong enemy. He came to this conclusion at the close of 1942, when the German infantry remained mired in the mud and snow of the Russian steppes.

5. Having established contact with Hitler's High Command, Dulles conducted meetings in Bern with Nazi General Reinhold Gehlen, the head of German military intelligence.

6. Knowing that the defeat of the Third Reich was inevitable, Gehlen had concocted the idea of forming clandestine guerilla squads—composed of Hitler youth and die-hard fascist fanatics, as "stay-behind units." These units, Gehlen informed Dulles, would serve as a police force to ward off a post-war Soviet invasion.

7. Believing the Soviets planned a take-over of Germany and Western Europe at the conclusion of the war, Dulles became convinced that the OSS must reach out to these stay-behind armies in order to supply them with tactical and strategic assistance.

8. Members of the stay-behind armies were known as "gladiators," who were commissioned to ward-off Communist invaders in the great theater of post-war Europe. And the operation in which they were engaged was to be known as "Gladio," after the short swords that the Roman gladiators used to kill their opponents.

9. Gladio expanded to Italy, where OSS officials, including James Jesus Angleton, secured the participation of Prince Junio Valerio Borghese, the leader of Decima Flottiglia MAS (10th Light Flotilla), better known as X MAS, an Italian naval commando unit.

10. Under Borghese, the Gladio forces in Italy were divided into forty main groups: ten specialized in sabotage; six in espionage, propaganda, and escape tactics; and twelve in guerilla activities.

11. A special training camp for members of the stay-behind units was set up in Sardinia, off Italy's western coast. The camp, thanks to the efforts of Gehlen and Wolff, was soon swarming with new gladiators from Germany, France, and Austria.

12. But there was a problem that seemed insurmountable. Gladio was a covert operation that had not been initiated by an act of Congress or a mandate from the Pentagon. Few federal officials knew of its existence. The $200 million in original funding came primarily from the House of Rockefeller since Gladio was to pave the way for a new world government under the control of the money cartel

13. A new and steady stream of revenue had to be created almost overnight since the operation would come to cost billions of dollars. But where could the cartel secure such a source of funding? The answer came from Paul E. Helliwell, who was serving as the OSS Chief of Special Intelligence in China.

DISCUSSION

A. How did the Office of Strategic Services come to represent an extension of the Society of the Elect?

_____

_____

_____

_____

B. How did Allen Dulles become a pivotal figure in the formation of the deep state?

_____

_____

_____

C. Why did Dulles seek a separate peace with Nazi Germany?

_____

_____

_____

_____

D. Who were the werewolves? How were they used by Dulles?

_____

_____

_____

_____

E. Discuss the purpose of Operation Gladio.

_____

_____

_____

_____

F. Why was it necessary for Gladio to extend into Italy?

_____

_____

_____

_____

G. How did the creation of Gladio give rise to an insurmountable problem for the newly created Central Intelligence Agency?

_____

_____

_____

_____

24

PRODUCING THE PLAGUE

1. In Kunming, a town within the South China province of Yunnan, Paul E. Helliwell, the OSS chief in China, observed that General Chiang Kai-Shek, leader of the Kuomintang (KMT), sold opium to Chinese addicts in order to raise funds for his army's planned war against the Communist forces of Mao Zedong.

2. Since his task was to provide covert assistance to the KMT, what better help could Helliwell provide than steady shipments of opiates for the good general from the U.S. military fleet of planes known as the Flying Tigers?

3. Delighted with the concept, General Wild Bill Donovan, the OSS director, arranged to funnel money to Helliwell, who now "became the man who controlled the pipe line of covert funds for secret operations throughout Asia."

4. This expenditure, from funds provided by Rockefeller, was approved by J.P. Morgan, Jr., who was in charge of the OSS finances, and James Warburg, son of Paul (the founder of the Federal Reserve), who served as Donovan's special assistant. Therefore, the involvement of the international banking establishment in the heroin venture was evident from the time of its inception.

5. Knowing of the plans to create a post-war intelligence agency that became known as the CIA, Helliwell came up with a sure-fire means of gaining covert funding for Gladio and other security operations. The new agency, he realized, could obtain cold cash by adopting the same measures of General Chiang. It could supply heroin to blacks in America's ghettos.

6. World War II had disrupted international shipping and imposed tight waterfront security that made smuggling of heroin into the United States almost impossible. Heroin supplies were small and international crime syndicates fell into disarray.

7. But opiates were becoming the rage of the jazz scene in Harlem, and the demand for China White was increasing day by day among black musicians in New York, where a hit could cost as much as $100.

8. Selling smack to the black jazz subculture would provide U.S. intelligence with a steady supply of revenue for Gladio throughout the post-war era. The Truman Administration had set aside no funds for covert, post-war operations in the federal budget. And cold cash alone could provide the means to purchase the services of foreign agents, foreign politicians, and foreign assassins without the approval of any elected official.

9. Working with Lucky Luciano and members of the Italian Mafia, the CIA secured two hundred kilos of heroin for the test run in America's inner cities from Schiaparelli, one of Italy's most respected pharmaceutical companies.

10. The Helliwell plan got underway at the close of the year and met with incredible success. The future of Gladio and other covert ventures was no longer in jeopardy. Helliwell's analysis had been correct. The jazz clubs were the perfect spots to peddle the product.

11. The shadow government now possessed sufficient funds not only to sustain secret armies throughout Europe but also to conduct covert operations throughout the world without public scrutiny.

DISCUSSION

A. Discuss the pivotal role that Paul E. Helliwell played in the creation of the international heroin trade.

_____

_____

_____

_____

B. What was the role of the international bankers in the Helliwell plan?

_____

_____

_____

_____

C. What was Civil Air Transport? How did it serve to develop the poppy fields of Southeast Asia?

_____

_____

_____

_____

D. What was the CIA's original source of funding for its covert operations?

_____

_____

_____

_____

E. Why was the black community singled out for the heroin experiment?

_____

_____

_____

_____

F. Why did the CIA need the services of Lucky Luciano and the Italian Mafia?

_____

_____

_____

_____

G. Discuss the way in which the heroin trade in the United States was protected.

_____

_____

_____

_____

PART SEVEN

ENDLESS ENTANGLEMENTS

John F. Kennedy held a dinner in the White House for a group of the brightest minds in the nation at that time. He made this statement: "This is perhaps the assembly of the most intelligence ever to gather at one time in the White House with the exception of when Thomas Jefferson dined alone."

"Fundamental Bible-believing people do not have the right to indoctrinate their children in their religious beliefs because we, the state, are preparing them for the year 2000, when America will be part of a one-world global society and their children will not fit in."

—NEBRASKA STATE SENATOR PETER HOAGLAND, SPEAKING ON RADIO IN 1983.

"My reading of history convinces me that most bad government results from too much government."

—THOMAS JEFFERSON

25

A CANCEROUS GROWTH

1. The United Nations, as conceived by the Council on Foreign Relations and funded by the House of Rockefeller, was designed to become an international regime that would control the world's weapons, its wars, its courts, its tax collectors, and its economy.

2. The most glaring problem with the United Nations Resolution, which was signed into law by President Harry S. Truman on July 28, 1945, was that it represented a treaty between the United States and a world governing organization. By law, a treaty can only be established between two sovereign nations, and the new organization was neither sovereign nor a state.

3. Another problem was that the treaty called upon the United States to engage in military action at the discretion of foreign governments. This violated the Constitution, which mandated that Congress alone possessed the power to declare war.

4. A third problem came with the Constitutional stipulation that the President of the United States remain the supreme commander-in-chief of the military in times of peace, with the ability to engage, at any time, America's armed forces in military conflict.

5. The center source of power within the United Nations resides with the Security Council. This council consists of five permanent member-nations—the United States, the United Kingdom France, Russia, and China. Any one of these member-nations possesses veto power over the final determinations. This relegation of power gives the organization a semblance of check and balance

6. But semblance is not reality, and the real control resides with the money cartel, who can force member-nations, even Russia, to comply with its interests since it possesses control over their economies. This control became evident on June 27, 1950, when the Security Council adopted Resolution 83 which determined that the attack on the Republic of Korea by Communist forces from North Korea constituted a "breach of peace" that warranted an immediate show of force.

7. Truman responded to the invasion by turning to the United Nations for a deployment of its peace-keeping force. It was a bit of a ruse since American soldiers comprised 85 percent of this force. The ruse was compounded when the Security Council voted to approve the deployment, even though the war could have been prevented if the Soviets had exercised their veto. But the Soviets were not present at the critical meeting.

8. The Korean War also produced a windfall for the American holdings of the money cartel, including the Rockefeller family. It necessitated a permanent military-industrial establishment in peacetime as well as in wartime.

9. Since the war mandated a quadrupling in military spending, the fortunes of the Rockefellers and the other global banking families increased exponentially. The Rockefellers had heavily invested in Boeing, McDonnell Aircraft, and other leading firms that received lucrative contracts with the Department of Defense. In addition to its oil companies (Exxon, Mobil, Texaco, Atlantic-Richfield, Standard Oil of California, Standard Oil of Indiana, and Marathon), the family had acquired majority control in steel companies (Inland Steel, Wheeling-Pittsburgh Steel, and National Steel) and chemical companies (Merck, Pfizer, and Wyeth), all of which reaped enormous profits from the so-called "police action."

10. The UN strategy involved the "mass killing of civilians" through extensive bombings. By the time an armistice was signed on July 27, 1953, a third of the population of North Korea—over 3 million people—had been wiped out.

11. The struggle resulted neither in territorial gain or loss. The objective of the war had been "containment," not liberation or victory. The terms of the armistice called for the creation of a demilitarized zone (DMZ) between North and South Korea. Each side was to be 2,200 yards from the center. The DMZ was to be patrolled by both sides at all times.

12. And so, it had come to this: America's wars were to be waged with limited rules of engagement and indefinite outcomes to advance the purpose of the global bankers, who had brought the United Nations into being.

13. Lucis Trust became an official consultative agency of the UN and its publishing arm. It was founded in 1922 as the Lucifer Publishing Company by Alice Bailey, a disciple of Helena Petrova Blavatsky. Blavatsky's works had a great impact on the thought of Cecil Rhodes.

14. Bailey's ultimate objective in establishing Lucis Trust was to bring about a one-world religion under the guiding light of Lucifer. She wrote: "The day is dawning when all religions will be regarded as emanating from one spiritual source; all will be seen as providing the one root out of which the universal religion will inevitably emerge."

DISCUSSION

A. What is the purpose of the United Nations?

_____

_____

_____

_____

B. How was the Council on Foreign Relations instrumental in the creation of the United Nations?

_____

_____

_____

_____

C. Discuss the treaty between the United Nations and the United States. Why is the treaty in violation of the Constitution?

_____

_____

_____

_____

D. Why did the Soviet Union fail to veto the Korean War?

_____

_____

_____

_____

E. How did the House of Rockefeller benefit from the Korean War?

_____

_____

_____

_____

F. Discuss the effects of the Korean War and the creation of the DMZ.

_____

_____

_____

_____

G. How did the Korean War give rise to a permanent military-industrial establishment?

_____

_____

_____

_____

H. What is the Lucis Trust?

_____

_____

_____

_____

I. How is the Lucis Trust related to Rhodes and Luciferianism?

_____

_____

_____

_____

26

THE EVIL SISTERS

1. In addition to the United Nations, the Council on Foreign Relations, through its War and Peace Studies Project, also spawned the International Monetary Fund (IMF) and the World Bank. The Articles of Agreement for these organizations were drawn up at an international conference of forty-four allied countries in Bretton Woods, New Hampshire. The agreement which brought the two sisters to life was ratified on December 27, 1945.

President Richard Nixon
The plan to wean the world from gold came to fruition on August 15, 1971, when President Richard Nixon signed an executive order declaring that the United States no longer would redeem its paper for gold.

2. The IMF, with headquarters in Washington, D.C., was set-up to "control international exchange rates" and to "stabilize currencies." The funding for the organization was based on a quota system with the most industrialized countries providing the greatest share of revenue. But the lion's share (over 20 percent came from the United States since the currencies of other countries were not transferable into gold.

3. The result of this arrangement was the ongoing transference of America's wealth to overseas banks, and the recognition of the dollar as the basis of the global economy.

4. As long as the dollar remained redeemable in gold, the amount of currency that could be created by the money cartel in charge of the IMF remained limited.

5. The plan to wean the world from gold came to fruition on August 15, 1971, when President Richard Nixon signed an executive order declaring that the United States no longer would redeem its paper dollars for gold.

6. Thanks to Nixon's executive order, the IMF now could function as the world's central bank by providing an unlimited issue of its own fiat currency to member nations. This new money, based solely on the money cartel's statement of its worth, was called a Special Drawing Right (SDR).

7. Nations borrow SDRs primarily to pay interest on their mounting debts. This would be fine and dandy, save for the fact that the IMF charges interest on every SDR that it produces from its computer system. And so, the loans do not serve to bolster failing economies. They simply create a steady flow of wealth from borrowing nations to the money changers who control the IMF and are not subject to any international supervision.

8. The dollar, severed from the gold standard, ceased to serve as the official IMF currency and was compelled to compete with other currencies—primarily the mark and the yen—on its relative value to the countries. For this reason, the dollar became increasingly discounted.

9. The dollar remained a favored medium of exchange since America as a country remained wide open to foreign investors. For this reason, the Federal Reserve continued to churn out massive amounts of fiat paper money, since the demand for such dollars seemed to be endless.

10. This situation permitted Americans to finance its enormous trade deficits with more and more money made out of nothing and allowed them to purchase cars, cell phones, computers, clothing generic drugs, and 70-inch high-definition television sets at cut-rate prices, while the foreign manufacturers got the greenbacks.

11. By the 21st century, this flood of dollars, which continued to be discounted, caused inflation to raise its hoary head until America was rapidly approaching the time when foreign manufacturers would no longer accept dollars for their goods and the Federal Reserve would no longer be able to finance its enormous trade deficit by churning out paper money.

12. While the IMF purportedly provides loans to stabilize economies, the World Bank, which was set up with funds from Morgan Stanley and First Boston (another J.P. Morgan facility), shelled out loans to war-ravaged and underdeveloped nations.

13. Through the years, the majority of the presidents of the World Bank have come from the stables of the Council on Foreign Relations.

14. The House of Morgan looked upon the World Bank as its greatest creation. It represented the crystallization of the family's efforts, beginning with the Pilgrim Society and the Federal Reserve, to acquire, along with the Rothschilds and the Rockefellers, ultimate control over the world's financial systems.

15. The World Bank established its headquarters in Washington, D.C. Its membership consisted of the same forty-four nations that belonged to the IMF. Like its sister agency, it was controlled by one-dollar, one-vote rather than the one country, one vote system of the UN. Since the United States provided nearly 20 percent of the money required to fund the World Bank, the New York bankers (Morgan, Rockefeller, and Kuhn-Loeb) gained a permanent place among the Bank's executive directors and the exclusive right to appoint the Bank president.

16. The World Bank was supposed to serve as the savior of mankind by enabling foreign governments to provide care for those most in need. The loans were provided on generous terms, usually at rates below market, and for durations as long as fifty years. The lion's share of the cash came from U.S. taxpayers.

17. But there is a snare to the World Bank's every transaction. The money, like IMF loans, is provided with very exacting conditions, known as structural-adjustment programs (SAPs).

18. One SAP is the immediate reimbursement to the country's creditors, such as Morgan Stanley, Chase Manhattan and Citibank. Another is the borrowing country's agreement to sell off its key assets, including its water supply, its pipelines, and its power systems to buyers provided by the World Bank/IMF. A third condition is the country's commitment to take remedial steps, including a restructuring of its government and the resettlement of populations, as dictated by World Bank/IMF officials.

19. Other SAP mandates include the lowering of existing wages, the raising of the interest rate, the downsizing of all state facilities, the phasing out of statutory minimal wages, and the termination of "surplus" teachers and health care workers. In extreme circumstances, even the resettlement of existing populations is required.

20. According to a three-year study by the Structural Adjustment Participatory Review International Network (SAPRIN), in collaboration with the World Bank, SAPs have been "expanding poverty, inequality, and insecurity around the world. They have torn at the heart of economies and the social fabric . . . increasing tensions among different social strata, fueling extremist movements and delegitimizing democratic political systems. Their effects, particularly on the poor, are so profound and pervasive that no amount of targeted social investments can begin to address the social crises that they have engendered."

21. Since the World Bank and the IMF are located in Washington, D.C., and controlled by the Houses of Morgan and Rockefeller, the people who have been subjected to SAPs manifest a strong anti-American animus. They assume that the twin banks are part of a corrupt capitalistic government that seeks to deprive them of life's basic necessities. Within forty years of the creation of these sister organizations, violent riots—directed against Americans and caused by the austerity programs—erupted in Argentina, Bolivia, Brazil, Ecuador, Egypt, Haiti, Liberia, Peru, and the Sudan.

DISCUSSION

A. What is the purpose of the International Monetary Fund (IMF)?

_____

_____

_____

_____

B. How is the IMF funded?

_____

_____

_____

_____

C. What is a bancor? How does it represent a nail in Uncle Sam's coffin?

_____

_____

_____

_____

D. How does the IMF function as the world's central bank?

_____

_____

_____

_____

E. Discuss the impact on international finance of Nixon's decision to remove the United States from the gold standard.

_____

_____

_____

_____

F. What is a Special Drawing Right (SDR)? How does it function?

_____

_____

_____

_____

G. How does the IMF contribute to the devaluation of the dollar?

_____

_____

_____

_____

H. Why does the dollar remain a favored means of exchange?

_____

_____

_____

_____

I. Why is the dollar unstable and how could its instability lead to the collapse of the American economy?

_____

_____

_____

_____

J. What is the purpose of the World Bank?

_____

_____

_____

_____

K. How did the World Bank come under the control of the House of Morgan?

_____

_____

_____

_____

L. Discuss the structural adjustment programs (SAPs) and how these programs have produced a hatred of the United States.

_____

_____

_____

_____

M. How did the SAPs impact the economies of such African countries as Tanzania, Uganda, and Zimbabwe?

_____

_____

_____

_____

THE DEATH KNELL

On August 15, 1971, President Richard M. Nixon removed the dollar from the gold standard, thereby allowing the International Monetary Fund (IMF) and the World Bank to gain control of the world's currencies. The IMF produces money out of nothing to "stabilize" the world's economy, while the World Bank provides onerous loans with interest to seize natural resources, including water supplies. The death knell for Uncle Sam tolled when these two organizations were spawned by the Council on Foreign Relations and the Houses of Morgan and Rockefeller.

27

THE BASTARD SON

1. The Central Intelligence Agency (CIA) was created in 1947 under the National Security Act to carry out covert operations "against hostile foreign states or groups or in support of friendly foreign states or groups but which are so planned and conducted that any U.S. government responsibility for them is not evident to unauthorized persons."

2. The ties between the new agency and the House of Rockefeller were apparent from the start. Top secret planning meetings were held at the Pratt House, the CFR headquarters in New York. These meetings were chaired by Allen Dulles, who, in 1947, remained a partner in Sullivan and Cromwell, the New York law firm that represented the Rockefeller business interests, and served as the CFR president.

3. The Agency would serve the interest of the Rockefellers and the money cartel by toppling foreign governments, seizing natural resources, promoting free trade, and opening channels of communication between the world's central banks.

4. In time, several of the CIA's covert operations, including MK-Ultra, would be funded by the Rockefeller family and the Rockefeller Foundation.

5. The first concern of the new intelligence agency was the situation in Italy, where the Italian Communist Party (*Partito Comunista Italiano*, or PCI) was poised to take control of the Italian government.

6. The heightened paranoia over the possibility of a PCI victory gave rise to the creation of the Office of Policy Coordination within the new intelligence agency. This office was authorized to engage in "paramilitary operations as well as political and economic warfare." The authorization for such covert action was included in a catch-all clause to the National Security Act of 1947 which granted the CIA the right to engage in "functions" related to "intelligence affecting the national security."

7. In the months before the 1948 national election, the CIA dumped $65 million of its black money into the Vatican Bank.

8. The heroin, which remained the source for the black money, continued to be supplied by Schiaparelli, the Italian pharmaceutical giant. The smack was sold within America's inner cities with the CIA believing that the drug epidemic would remain confined to the lowest strata of society.

9. One year after the election, renewed fears of a Communist take-over of Italy arose from Stalin's creation of the *Comecon*, the union of the Soviet Union, Bulgaria, Czechoslovakia, Hungary, Poland, and Romania, to enforce the Soviet dominion of the lesser states of central Europe.

10. In the face of this development, the CIA opted to extend support for the Christian Democratic Party in Italy and stay-behind units throughout Western Europe with billions in covert funding that could only come from the expansion of the drug trade.

11. The CIA funds were deposited in Catholic banks throughout Italy, including *Banco Ambrosiano*. These banks, thanks to the Lateran Treaty, were safe from scrutiny by the Bank of Italy and Italy's treasury department.

12. The Christian Democratic Party, the official political party of the Roman Catholic Church, continued to receive more than $20 million in annual aid from the Agency, and, in return, the CIA established a "Vatican desk" under James Jesus Angleton.

DISCUSSION

A. Why was the Central Intelligence Agency (CIA) created?

_____

_____

_____

_____

B. How was the CIA linked to the House of Rockefeller?

_____

_____

_____

_____

C. Discuss the recruiting procedure of the new agency and how this procedure furthered the interests of the deep state.

_____

_____

_____

_____

D. Why was the CIA so concerned with the rise of the Italian Communist Party in 1947?

_____

_____

_____

_____

E. How did the CIA make use of the Italian Mafia?

_____

_____

_____

_____

F. How was heroin imported into the United States during the postwar period?

_____

_____

_____

_____

G. How did the CIA make use of Catholic banks in Italy?

_____

_____

_____

_____

H. What is the Christian Democratic Party? Discuss the ties of the Christian Democrats to the Vatican, the Mafia, and the CIA.

_____

_____

_____

_____

I. What was the necessity for the CIA to establish a Vatican Desk?

_____

_____

_____

_____

28

ONSLAUGHT OF ATROCITIES

1. Not wanting to be dependent on Schiaparelli, the Italian pharmaceutical giant, for the heroin to mount ongoing covert operations, the CIA worked with General Chiang Kai-Shek and his Kuomintang (KMT) army to create a drug route that would lead from Southeast Asia to the United States.

2. By 1951, the CIA began supplying arms and materiel to the KMT troops, whose sole activity was opium cultivation. This venture became the second example of the CIA conducting off-the-books foreign policy with assets of which the American people and most elected officials remained completely unaware.

3. The decisions concerning this policy were made within the Office of Policy Coordination by a very small group of elite intelligence officials whose parameters remained undefined. These officials served America's rising "military industrial complex" which relied on privatized military and intelligence contractors, international bankers, and even Washington's most highly organized lobbyists.

4. To expedite the arms-for-drugs venture in the Far East, William Donovan, the former head of OSS, resigned from the military to form the World Commerce Corporation (WCC) with a small group of very wealthy friends, including Nelson Rockefeller, Joseph C. Grew (nephew of J.P. Morgan), Alfred DuPont, and Charles Jocelyn Hambro, director of the Hambros Bank and The Bank of England with close ties to the Morgan family.

5. The opium was flown from the mountains of Burma and Laos by Cargo Air Transport to Bangkok, where the planes were emptied and loaded with weapons for the return flight to the poppy fields.

6. As the Western World became increasingly inundated with heroin, the CIA, through spokesmen such as George White of the Federal Bureau of Narcotics (FBN), placed the blame on Chairman Mao and the People's Republic of China, who were accused of orchestrating the movement of 200–400 tons of opium per year from Yunnan to Bangkok. Such reports represented the first unfurling of a CIA false flag.

7. Knowing the importance of issuing such false reports, the CIA, under Allen Dulles, initiated Operation Mockingbird in 1953. This operation consisted of the recruitment of leading journalists and editors to fabricate stories and to create smokescreens in order to cast the Agency's agenda in a positive light.

8. In 1953, the CIA turned its attention to Tehran, when the Iranian Prime Minister Mohammed Mosaddegh nationalized the Anglo-Persian Oil Company. By purchasing the services of Iranian journalists, military officers, and members of parliament, the Agency was able to spread false reports that Mosaddegh was Jewish and a Communist. After Mosaddegh was arrested and tossed out of office, the CIA replaced him with Mohammad Reza Pahlavi, the Shah of Iran. The oil industry was de-nationalized, and the country's national treasure was handed over to companies owned or partially owned by the House of Rockefeller.

9. Inspired by North Korea's brainwashing program, the CIA launched its own experiments on mind control in an operation known as MK-Ultra. The project involved giving massive infusions of hallucinogens, including LSD, to American subjects without their knowledge or against their will. Funded by the Rockefeller and Ford Foundations, MK-Ultra also included studies of means of controlling the thoughts of the American people through public relations, advertising, hypnosis, and other forms of suggestion.

10. In Guatemala, the CIA overthrew the democratically-elected Jacob Arbenz in a military coup. Arbenz threatened to nationalize the Rockefeller-owned United Fruit Company, of which CIA Director Allen Dulles was a shareholder.

11. Radio Free Europe, a CIA propaganda outlet, incited Hungary to revolt by broadcasting Soviet premier Nikita Khrushchev's Secret Speech, in which he denounced his predecessor Josef Stalin. The conflict resulted in the deaths of 7,000 Soviets and 30,000 Hungarians. The propaganda spewed from Radio Free Europe was so blatantly false that it was illegal to publish transcripts of the broadcasts in the United States.

12. With the assistance of the U.S. military, "Papa Doc" Duvalier became dictator of Haiti. He created his own private police force, the "Tonton Macoutes," who terrorized the population with machetes. When Papa Doc died in 1971, his 19-year-old son, called "Baby Doc," became "president-for-life."

13. In 1960, the Gladio operation turned strategic, when the Turkish stay-behind unit, known as Counter-Guerilla, joined with the military to stage a coup d'état against the government of Prime Minister Adnan Menderes. Menderes, who was planning a visit to Moscow to secure economic aid, was cast into prison, put on trial by a hastily assembled court, and executed at the gallows on the island of Imrali.

14. The Association for Responsible Dissent estimates that by 1987, six million people had died as a result of CIA covert operations. Former State Department official William Blum correctly calls this an "American Holocaust."

15. When these atrocities took place, Dwight David Eisenhower occupied the Oval Office. Like FDR, Ike had been groomed for the presidency by the Council on Foreign Relations.

16. During his eight years in office, Ike advanced the demise of the country by halting the Reece Committee's investigation of the control tax-exempt foundations wielded over America's educational, cultural, and religious institutions—by producing national deficits that were five times greater than Harry Truman's, by promoting the growth of the military-industrial complex by unchecked defense spending, and by crushing the Bricker Amendment, which stipulated that no treaty signed by the U.S. could override the Constitution or infringe on the rights of American citizens.

17. Even more alarming was the Eisenhower Administration's production of a State Department document called *Freedom from War—The U.S. Program for General and Complete Disarmament* which proposed that America should surrender all its weapons, including its nuclear arsenals, to the United Nations.

DISCUSSION

A. What necessitated the U.S. presence in Southeast Asia?

_____

_____

_____

_____

B. Discuss the function of the World Commerce and Cargo Air Transport.

_____

_____

_____

_____

C. What is Operation Mockingbird? Why is this operation so essential to the deep state?

_____

_____

_____

_____

D. Why did the CIA become involved in Iran?

_____

_____

_____

_____

E. Why did the CIA stage a military coup in Guatemala?

_____

_____

_____

_____

F. How does Radio Free Europe serve the interest of the shadow government?

_____

_____

_____

_____

G. Why is Turkey a pivotal concern of the CIA?

_____

_____

_____

_____

H. Discuss Dwight David Eisenhower's (Ike's) ties to the Council on Foreign Relations.

_____

_____

_____

_____

I. What was the impact of the Dulles brothers on the course of U.S. history?

_____

_____

_____

_____

J. How did Ike contribute to the demise of the Uncle Sam?

_____

_____

_____

_____

PART EIGHT

THE POINT OF NO RETURN

At five, began studying under his cousin's tutor.

At nine, studied Latin, Greek, and French.

At fourteen, studied classical literature and additional languages.

At sixteen, entered the College of William and Mary.

At nineteen, studied law for five years starting under George Wythe.

At twenty-three, started his own law practice.

At twenty-five, was elected to the Virginia House of Burgesses.

At thirty-one, wrote the widely circulated "Summary View of the Rights of British America" and retired from his law practice.

At thirty-two, was a Delegate to the Second Continental Congress.

At thirty-three, wrote the Declaration of Independence.

At thirty-three, took three years to revise Virginia's legal code and wrote a Public Education bill and a statute for Religious Freedom.

At thirty-six, was elected the second Governor of Virginia, succeeding Patrick Henry.

At forty, served in Congress for two years.

At forty-one, was the American minister to France and negotiated commercial treaties with European nations along with Ben Franklin and John Adams. At forty-six, served as the first secretary of state under George Washington.

At fifty-three, served as vice-president and was elected president of the American Philosophical Society.

At fifty-five, drafted the Kentucky Resolutions and became the active head of Republican Party.

At fifty-seven, was elected the third president of the United States. At sixty, obtained the Louisiana Purchase, doubling the nation's size.

At sixty-one, was elected to a second term as president.

At sixty-five, retired to Monticello.

At eighty, helped President Monroe shape the Monroe Doctrine.

At eighty-one, almost single-handedly created the University of Virginia and served as its first president.

At eighty-three, died on the fiftieth anniversary of the signing of the Declaration of Independence.

29

THE NEW FRONTIER

1. Under John F. Kennedy, the key cabinet positions remained occupied by officials from the Council on Foreign Relations. Dean Rusk, the president of the Rockefeller Foundation, became Secretary of State; C. Douglas Dillon, the future CFR vice chairman and former member of the Eisenhower cabinet, became Secretary of the Treasury. And Robert Strange McNamara, Ford Motor Company president and future president of the World Bank, became Secretary of Defense.

John F. Kennedy
JFK was a socialist who belonged to the Fabian Society, an internationalist who sanctioned the surrender of all arms (including nukes) to the United Nations, and a supporter of the IMF/World Bank.

2. The Kennedy record was characterized by political embarrassment and executive indecision. He launched the Bay of Pigs invasion of Cuba under a group of 1,400 Cuban expatriates and, at the last minute, failed to provide the force with necessary air support, thereby dooming the mission to failure.

3. To resolve the Cuban Missile Crisis, Kennedy did not confront Nikita Khrushchev with steadfast resolve. Instead, he acquiesced to the Soviet premier's demand that the U.S. remove all of its intermediate range missile bases in England, Italy, and Turkey.

4. Under Kennedy's three-year watch, the CIA launched 163 covert operations, only seven fewer than similar undertakings under the eight years of Eisenhower.

5. JFK was a socialist who belonged to the Fabian Society, an internationalist who sanctioned the surrender of all arms (including nukes) to the United Nations, and a supporter of the IMF/World Bank.

6. The Rockefeller animosity arose from Kennedy's "Alliance for Progress," which he launched on March 13, 1961. This program provided massive amounts of foreign aid to Latin America. The $1.4 billion in annual aid was supposed to stimulate economic growth, redistribute wealth, and promote democratic governments. The Bolivian and Chilean governments were encouraged to use their share of the aid to purchase equipment for the nationalization of mines throughout the country, including the very lucrative tin, silver, and copper mines owned by the Rockefellers. In Peru and Venezuela, the money was used to prop up state-run oil companies, much to the detriment of Standard Oil.

7. The "Alliance for Progress" program, which threatened the enormous interest of the House of Rockefeller south of the border, was followed by Kennedy's mishandling of the Bay of Pigs invasion which resulted in Castro expropriating the Standard Oil refinery in Cuba and other Rockefeller holdings.

8. After launching his Latin American program, Kennedy appeared before the American Newspaper Publishers Association to deliver a speech that may have sealed his fate. In a veiled reference to the House of Rockefeller and the money cartel, he spoke of a "monolithic and ruthless conspiracy" that sought to rule the world.

9. With Executive Order #11110, Kennedy instructed the Treasury Department—rather than the Federal Reserve—"to issue silver certificates against any silver bullion, silver, or silver dollars in the Treasury." This meant that for every ounce of silver in the U.S. Treasury's vault, the government could introduce new money, with actual value, into circulation.

10. In compliance with this order, United States Notes in the amount of $4,292,893,815 were produced in $2 and $5 denominations. This was not fiat money. It was paper currency with actual value. And, since it was issued by the government rather than the Fed, the money came interest-free.

11. Kennedy, with one stroke of the pen, threatened to put the Federal Reserve out of business. The Fed no longer could manipulate the economy by producing and withholding money. It no longer could create depression or prosperity. It no longer could manufacture money from nothing. And the money cartel, including the House of Rockefeller, no longer could exact billions in interest for lending the money to pay off the national debt.

12. In the wake of Kennedy's assassination on November 22, 1963, no more silver certificates were issued and no other American president dared to defy the Fed and its secret shareholders.

13. The wife of Lee Harvey Oswald, who was conveniently gunned down by Jack Ruby before Ruby himself was shot, told author A.J. Weberman in 1994, "The answer to the Kennedy assassination is with the Federal Reserve Bank. Don't underestimate that. It's wrong to blame it on Angleton and the CIA per se only. This is only one finger on the same hand. The people who supply the money are above the CIA."

DISCUSSION

A. Discuss the Bay of Pigs invasion.

_____

_____

_____

_____

B. What was the stance of JFK during the Cuban Missile Crisis?

_____

_____

_____

_____

C. How was Kennedy responsible for the war in Vietnam?

_____

_____

_____

_____

D. What is the Fabian Society? Discuss its appeal to JFK.

_____

_____

_____

_____

E. How did JFK gain the enmity of the House of Rockefeller?

_____

_____

_____

_____

F. Discuss Kennedy's Address to the American Newspaper Publishers Association.

_____

_____

_____

_____

G. What was Executive Order #11110? How did it threaten the existence of the Federal Reserve?

_____

_____

_____

_____

H. Discuss the Kennedy assassination. What are the arguments against the single-assassin theory?

_____

_____

_____

_____

THE FAMILY THAT KEEPS ON KILLING

The Rockefeller family was not only instrumental in the creation of the Council on Foreign Relations, the United Nations, the International Monetary Fund, the World Bank, the Trilateral Commission, the East-West Trade Agreement, the granting of "most favored nation" trade status to China, and the North American Free Trade Agreement (NAFTA), but also played a significant role in the spread of the plague of heroin, the legalization of abortion, the "demythology" of the New Testament, and, possibly, even the assassination of John F. Kennedy.

30

A HELL OF A HOAX

1. On August 4, 1964, all nationally televised programs were interrupted for this urgent message from U.S. President Lyndon B. Johnson: "My fellow Americans: As President and Commander in Chief, it is my duty to the American people to report that renewed hostile actions against United States ships on the high seas in the Gulf of Tonkin have today required me to order the military forces of the United States to take action in reply."

2. The next morning, Johnson appeared before Congress to gain the approval for direct military involvement in the Vietnam Civil War. The resolution was passed by a vote of 416 to 0 in the House and 88 to 2 in the Senate.

Lyndon B. Johnson
President Johnson appointed a CFR member to virtually every strategic position in his administration.

3. The country was now involved in a war that would lead to over 50,000 American deaths and millions of Vietnamese casualties. The official story of the cause remained the same throughout the course of the war. North Vietnamese torpedo boats launched an "unprovoked attack" against a U.S. destroyer on "routine patrol" in the Tonkin Gulf on August 2 — and two days later, North Vietnamese PT boats launched a torpedo attack on two U.S. destroyers in another act of unwarranted aggression. But there was a problem. It was all a hoax. The sailors really were shooting at flying fish. The second attack never happened.

4. The overall policy of the Vietnam War, as developed by George Keenan, Dean Acheson, and other CFR officials, was "containment," the attempt to confine the Communist countries to their existing borders. It was the same policy that failed in Korea. Containment implied limited warfare. Victory was not an objection, but rather a liability.

5. The Vietnam War was not only to be limited but also fought with extraordinary restrictions, known as "rules of engagement." These rules prohibited American soldiers from firing at the Viet Cong unless they were being fired upon, and, even when attacked, they were forbidden to pursue the enemy forces into Laos or Cambodia. In accordance with the same restrictions, American pilots could only bomb targets that were deemed "strategic" by the Joint Chiefs of Staff, and they were not allowed to destroy Viet Cong missile sites that were still under construction.

6. David Rockefeller met with Soviet premier Nikita Khrushchev in Moscow to draft a trade agreement that would extend most-favored nation status within the Soviet Communist bloc. Thanks to this treaty, 85 percent of the war materiel for the Viet Cong came from factories within the Soviet Union.

7. But more was at stake in Southeast Asia than the ideology of containment and the immediate opportunity to reap financial benefits from the conflict. The region produced the poppy crops that were becoming one of the world's most valuable commodities. Without the flow of heroin from the Golden Triangle of Burma, Laos, and Thailand, the funding for the CIA's covert operations, which opened new markets for the money cartel, would come to an abrupt halt.

8. By 1971, there were more than 500,000 heroin addicts in the U.S., producing a cash flow of $12 billion. Over three million Americans admitted on a government survey to using heroin at least once. Down at the morgue, where people don't lie, the numbers told a different story: 41 percent of the drug-related deaths were now linked to heroin.

9. Southeast Asia remained the main source of opium. From Laos alone, over a ton a month arrived in Saigon on C-47 military transport planes that had been provided by the CIA to Lt. General Vang Pao of the Royal Lao Army.

10. Some of this same heroin was smuggled into the United States in body bags containing dead soldiers.

DISCUSSION

A. Discuss the Gulf of Tonkin incident. Why would LBJ perpetuate a falsehood in order to drag the United States into the Vietnam Conflict?

_____

_____

_____

_____

B. What is the concept of "containment?"

_____

_____

_____

_____

C. Discuss the rationale for the Rules of Engagement.

_____

_____

_____

_____

D. Why was David Rockefeller so intent upon forging the East-West Trade Agreement?

_____

_____

_____

_____

E. What was the hidden agenda of the Vietnam War?

_____

_____

_____

_____

F. Discuss Operation Eagle and what this undertaking revealed about the international drug trade.

_____

_____

_____

_____

G. What accounts for the complacency of the American people before the drug epidemic?

_____

_____

_____

_____

H. Discuss the consequences of the drug trade on international banking.

_____

_____

_____

_____

THE BODY BAGS

The CIA's involvement in trafficking heroin was revealed by the bodies of dead American soldiers that were shipped from Vietnam to Andrews Air Force Base and other military installations within the United States. The bodies were eviscerated and stuffed with bags of heroin. When DEA agent Michael Levine attempted to bust this operation, he was warned off by his superiors since such action could result in the exposure of the supply line from Long Tieng.

31

THE BLACK BANK

1. The Nugan Hand Bank had been established in 1973. Shortly after setting up headquarters in Sydney, the bank blossomed into 22 branches. One branch was set up in Chiang Mai, the heart of Thailand's opium industry, in the same suite as the United States Drug Enforcement Administration (DEA). The DEA receptionist answered the bank's phone and took messages when the representatives were out.

2. The money taken from the bank by the CIA was used to purchase weapons from international arms dealer Edwin Wilson for guerilla forces in Indonesia, Thailand, Malaysia, Brazil, and the white Rhodesian government of Ian Smith.

3. The Nugan Hand Bank also imported heroin into Australia from the Golden Triangle.

4. The board of directors and administrative staff members of the Nugan Hand Bank represented a "Who's Who" of prominent CIA officials.

5. The primary shareholder of the Nugan Hand Bank was Australasian and Pacific Holding, a company that was owned and operated by the Rockefellers' Chase Manhattan Bank.

6. The proceeds from the heroin trade, as funneled through the Nugan Hand Bank, permitted the CIA to mount hundreds of covert operations throughout the world.

7. The operations of the Nugan Hand Bank came to a screeching halt with the fall of Saigon on April 30, 1975.

8. Saigon now became a dead end to Southeast Asia's drug traffic, thanks to the anti-drug policies of the Viet Cong. Crude opium still crossed the border from Laos to service the city's declining addict population, but choice-number-four heroin was no longer available.

9. Between 1978 and 1980, the Golden Triangle was hit with two severe droughts. The droughts were followed by two seasons of intense monsoon rains, which reduced the region's opium production to a record low. The usual 600-ton opium harvests were cut to 160 tons in 1978 and 240 tons in 1979.

10. New poppy fields had to be planted within countries that possessed the proper climate and terrain— cool plateaus above 500 feet. The CIA now set its sights on the fertile growing fields of Afghanistan.

11. The Vietnam War produced a massive new source of cheap labor for global industrialists. The recommended minimum wage for Vietnamese workers was the lowest in the world, amounting to $30 per month in 1994. There was a fortune to be made by relocating American manufacturing plants to the war-ravaged country, which began to produce such American brand-name clothing and shoes as Michael Kors, Dockers, Brooks Brothers, Rockport and Hanes underwear.

12. Companies such as Microsoft, Nike, Samsung Electronics, LG Group, Intel, Canon, Panasonic and Toshiba have constructed multi-billion dollar plants in Vietnam, thanks to funding from JPMorgan Chase of Ho Chi Minh City and Citibank Vietnam.

DISCUSSION

A. What was telling about the death of Frank Nugan?

_____

_____

_____

_____

B. Who was Michael Hand?

_____

_____

_____

_____

C. What was the need for the Nugan Hand Bank?

_____

_____

_____

_____

D. Discuss the CIA's involvement in the Nugan Hand Bank.

_____

_____

_____

_____

E. Discuss the involvement of the Rockefeller family in the Australian bank.

_____

_____

_____

_____

F. Why would the Rockefellers shell out money for college students to stage demonstrations?

_____

_____

_____

_____

G. Why was the House of Rockefeller so intent upon transforming the United States into a socialist country?

_____

_____

_____

_____

H. What brought about the collapse of the Nugan Hand Bank?

_____

_____

_____

_____

I. How did the fall of Saigon give rise to the war in Afghanistan?

_____

_____

_____

_____

J. What financial benefits were reaped by the money cartel from the Vietnam War?

_____

_____

_____

_____

PART NINE

THE FINAL CURTAIN

"The real rulers in Washington are invisible and exercise their power from behind the scenes."
—JUSTICE FELIX FRANKFURTER, U.S. SUPREME COURT. HE SERVED FROM
JANUARY 30, 1939, TO AUGUST 28, 1962.

"I believe that banking institutions are more dangerous to our liberties than standing armies. If the American people ever allow private banks to control the issue of their currency, first by inflation, then by deflation, the banks and corporations that will grow up around the banks will deprive the people of all property—until their children wake up homeless on the continent their fathers conquered."
—THOMAS JEFFERSON, 1802

"I am a most unhappy man. I have unwittingly ruined my country. A great industrial nation is controlled by its system of credit. Our system of credit is concentrated. The growth of the nation, therefore, and all our activities are in the hands of a few men. We have come to be one of the worst ruled, one of the most completely controlled and dominated Governments in the civilized world, no longer a Government by free opinion, no longer a Government by conviction and the vote of the majority, but a Government by the opinion and duress of a small group of dominant men."
—WOODROW WILSON, IN 1916, THREE YEARS AFTER SIGNING THE FEDERAL RESERVE
INTO EXISTENCE

"The tree of liberty must be refreshed from time to time with the blood of patriots and tyrants."
—THOMAS JEFFERSON

32

TRANSFORMING THE POPULATION

1. In 1965, aside from the temples of the Nation of Islam (an African-American religion sect that professed doctrines and beliefs version that bore no similarity to the teachings of the Prophet Mohammed), the only mosques in the United States were in Cedar Rapids, Iowa, Dearborn, Michigan, and Washington, D.C. (which opened in 1957)—and all three boasted fewer than 100 members. Four other cities contained miniature mosques with fewer than fifty members.

2. The absence of Muslims from the millions of immigrants was due to the restrictive immigration legislation that remained in effect to safeguard the racial and religious balance of America.

3. By 1924, the U.S. Congress closed the floodgates to the country and limited the annual flow of immigrants into the country to two percent of each nationality who lived in the country in 1890. The reliance of this legislation on the ethnic composition of the country before the turn of the century guaranteed that the majority of new arrivals would be from Northern Europe.

4. In 1952, The McCarran Walter Immigration Act affirmed the national-origins quota system of 1924 and limited total annual immigration to one-sixth of one percent of the population (175,455) of the continental United States in 1920.

5. The push for immigration reform came from two sources. The first was a group that consisted of influential Jewish congressmen and senators, including Emanuel Celler, Jacob Javits, and Herbert H. Lehman, whose efforts to eliminate the quota system were backed by such powerful Jewish organizations as the Anti-Defamation League, the American Jewish Committee, the National Council of Jewish Women, the Hebrew Aid Society, the Synagogue Council of America, B'nai B'rith, the Jewish Labor Committee, and the Jewish War Veterans of the United States.

6. A second source of the legislation were the thoughts of Count Richard Nicholas von Coudenhove-Kalergi, the son of an Austrian diplomat and Japanese heiress, who has been hailed as "the father of the European Union."

7. In his books *Praktischer Idealismus* and *Kampf im Paneuropa*, Coudenhove-Kalergi argued for the dissolution of national borders and the promotion of mass allogenic (genetically dissimilar) immigration. The result of this immigration, Coudenhove-Kalergi wrote, would be the creation of "the men of future," whom he called *mestizos*. Such men would be of mixed Caucasian, Negro, and Asiatic blood and would appear "very similar to the ancient Egyptians."

8. When France fell to Hitler's forces in 1940, Coudenhove-Kalergi made his way to the United States, where he came under the care of the Council on Foreign Relations (CFR). As an advisor to the group, he helped to draft the wartime strategy of the Office of Strategic Services and the postwar plans for the revitalization of Europe.

9. The Immigration and Naturalization Act of 1965 was supposed to serve as a symbolic gesture—an extension of civil rights sentiments—that would not produce a huge and sustained increase in the number of newcomers from Third World countries, let alone serve as a vehicle for globalizing immigration.

10. Opponents of the legislation argued that it would vastly increase the number of immigrants coming into the country and that the bulk of those immigrants would be coming from Third World nations, representing a threat to the country's existing demographic profile.

11. The House of Representatives voted 326 to 69 (82.5 percent) in favor of the act, while the Senate passed the bill by a vote of 76 to 18. The floodgates to the New World finally had been pried open.

12. The Rockefeller family throughout the decades remained fixated on other aspects of population redistribution and control, including matters of people planning.

13. On July 18, 1969, President Richard M. Nixon appointed John D. Rockefeller III as chairman of the newly created Commission on Population Growth and the American Future.

14. One of the first reports from the Commission recommended "that present state laws restricting abortion be liberalized along the lines of the New York State Statute, such abortions be performed on request by duly-licensed physicians under conditions of medical safety."

15. Thanks to this report, the New York model abortion law, which the Commission enthusiastically endorsed, was passed in 1970 under the leadership of New York Governor Nelson Rockefeller, John D. III's brother. This legislation, coupled with statements from the Commission, paved the way for *Roe v. Wade.*

16. By 2017, 59,115,995 babies had been aborted in a land once consecrated to Christian ideals.

DISCUSSION

A. Discuss Islam in America before 1965.

_____

_____

_____

_____

B. What was the quota system?

_____

_____

_____

_____

C. How was the quota system justified?

_____

_____

_____

_____

D. Why did influential Jewish senators and congressmen push for immigration reform?

_____

_____

_____

E. Who was Count Richard Nicholas von Coudenhove-Kalergi?

_____

_____

_____

_____

F. Discuss Coudenhove-Kalergi's concept of "men of the future."

_____

_____

_____

_____

G. How did Coudenhove-Kalergi come under the care of the Council on Foreign Relations?

_____

_____

_____

_____

H. Discuss the impact of Coudenhove-Kalergi's thought on prominent American thinkers, such as Susan Sontag.

_____

_____

_____

_____

I. How did Senator Edward Kennedy shepherd the Immigration and Naturalization Act of 1965 through the Senate?

_____

_____

_____

_____

J. Discuss the opposition to the immigration act.

_____

_____

_____

_____

K. Why were members of the Rockefeller family obsessed with the matter of population control?

_____

_____

_____

_____

L. How did John D. Rockefeller, III, pave the way for legalized abortion?

_____

_____

_____

_____

M. Can *Roe v. Wade* be repealed? Why? Why not?

_____

_____

_____

_____

THE FATHER OF THE EUROPEAN UNION AND HATRED OF WHITE AMERICA

In his books *Praktischer Idealismus* and *Kampf im Paneuropa*, Count Richard Nicholas von Coudenhove-Kalergi argued for the dissolution of national borders and the promotion of mass allogenic (genetically dissimilar) immigration. The result of this immigration, Coudenhove-Kalergi wrote, would be the creation of "the men of future," whom he called *mestizos*. Such men would be of mixed Caucasian, Negro, and Asiatic blood and would appear "very similar to the ancient Egyptians." The mongrelization of mankind, according to Coudenhove-Kalergi, would produce salubrious results, such as the dissolution of nationalism, the elimination of racism, and the eradication of disparities in levels of human intelligence.

Since the *mestizos* would be of limited intelligence, Coudenhove-Kalergi maintained, they could be easily manipulated and controlled by "Jewish leaders of socialism" (*herrenmenschen*), who had been singled out by divine providence to rule the world.

The ideas of the celebrated Austrian count gave rise not only to a unified Europe but also to the belief that the white race of Americans must be eradicated for the good of humanity. Susan Sontag, one of Coudenhove-Kalergi's admirers, penned these words in 1967 for *Partisan Review*: "*The white race is the cancer of human history; it is the white race and it alone—its ideologies and inventions—which eradicates autonomous civilizations wherever it spreads, which has upset the ecological balance of the planet, which now threatens the very existence of life itself.*"

33

ONLY THE DEAD KNOW BROOKLYN AND OTHER STORIES

1. In 1990, less than 600 mosques existed in the U.S. By 2012, that number climbed to 2,106. Nearly 8.5 percent of America's 330,000 houses of worship were now mosques.

2. A 2008 study by Cornell University projected that the number of Muslims in America had climbed from 1.6 million in 1995 to 7 million.

3. By 2010, the median mosque in America drew a crowd of three-hundred worshippers to its Friday service, while the average Christian church mustered a meager Sunday gathering of seventy-five.

Mosques
The Islamic boom was evidenced by reports of the new mosques and halal restaurants that had sprouted up within every major American city.

4. To come to terms with the social, political, economic, and religious impact of Islam on the U.S. landscape, you need only pay a visit to Brooklyn—the borough of New York City once known as "the all-American neighborhood." Such a visit will make you aware not only of the Islamic transformation of U.S. cities but also of the woeful inadequacies of religious statistics, especially those which pertain to mosques and the number of Muslims now residing within major metropolitan areas throughout the country.

5. Throughout Brooklyn, one can now hear the call of the *muezzin* five times a day from rooftop speakers: *Allahu akbar. Ashhadu an la ilaha illa-Llah.* Cab drivers pull their hacks to the side of the road and perform ritual ablutions. Shopkeepers roll out their prayer rugs toward the holy city. And life within the borough—which was once known as the "city of churches"—comes to a standstill.

6. Many Jews and Christians throughout Brooklyn now display American flags and an assortment of patriotic/jingoistic banners in their front yards. These displays, for the most part, are acts of defiance. "We're besieged," one resident told *The Jerusalem Post*. "Making a statement is all we can do. They aren't delighted to see the flag wave. This is enemy territory."

7. The vast majority of Muslim newcomers display an unwillingness to assimilate. They continue to wear Islamic attire, maintain *halal* diets, and rigidly comply with *sharia* law.

8. Few Muslim women walk the streets of Brooklyn without a head covering; some wear full *burqas* that conceal their bodies and *niqabs* that conceal their faces, leaving only mesh-covered slits for their eyes.

9. The assimilation process in Brooklyn appears to be working in reverse since the new male converts to Islam, almost all of whom are African-American, now wear skull caps and long white tunics (*shalwat kameezes*), while their wives walk several feet behind them in black *burqas* or *abaya* gowns. They dye their beards with henna; refrain from eating pork and drinking alcoholic beverages; and greet each other in Arabic (*As-Salāmu `Alaykum*).

10. Polygamy, among the newcomers and converts, is commonplace, and *khat*—the favorite narcotic of North African Muslims—is now cut up and sold on street corners, *halal* grocery shops, and places like the Blue Province Restaurant.

11. In crowded flats and make-shift clinics along Atlantic Avenue, young Muslim girls—some as young as two—are subjected to the practice of female genital mutilation. Dubbed "female circumcision," this practice consists of the removal of the clitoris without the benefit of anesthesia or surgical instruments. Broken bottles or tin can lids occasionally serve as scalpels. Recent statistics show that 41,000 Somali and other North African Muslims in Brooklyn and the other boroughs of New York City have been subjugated to this ordeal.

12. By 1989, the first North American cell of al-Khifa, an organization that would eventually morph into al-Qaeda, was implanted by Abdullah Azzam within Brooklyn's Masjid al-Farooq at 554 Atlantic Avenue. Members of this mosque came to play key roles in the assassination of Rabbi Meier Kahane, the 1993 bombing of the World Trade Center, and the planning of 9/11.

13. Brooklyn also gave birth to Dar ul-Islam, the nation's most notorious Islamic street gang; Jamaat ul-Fuqra, a Muslim group that had been responsible for thirty terror attacks on American soil, and the Albanian Mafia, which became the country's "leading crime outfit."

14. What has taken place in Brooklyn has occurred in major cities throughout the country—most notably, Detroit, Washington, D.C., Cedar Rapids, Philadelphia and Atlanta —and even quaint towns and villages, such as Lodi, California; Lewiston, Maine; Hancock, New York; Commerce, Georgia; and Hamtramck, Michigan.

DISCUSSION

A. What is America's current Muslim population? Discuss the uncertainty of statistics.

_____

_____

_____

_____

B. Discuss the impact on the rise of Islam on American's urban centers.

_____

_____

_____

_____

C. What accounts for the fact that Muslims as evidenced by mosque attendance in America remain fiercely committed to their faith, while the vast majority of Americans never darken the doorway of a church?

_____

_____

_____

_____

D. Why was Brooklyn once known as "the all-American" city?

_____

_____

_____

_____

E. What changes have taken place within Brooklyn in the past two decades?

_____

_____

_____

_____

F. Outline the reasons why Brooklyn emerged as a hotbed of homegrown terrorism.

_____

_____

_____

_____

G. Why is Islam so appealing to African-Americans?

_____

_____

_____

_____

H. What cities within the United States are becoming primarily Islamic? Why does this pose a threat to America as a nation?

_____

_____

_____

_____

I. Discuss the reasons why Muslims have been so reluctant to assimilate within American culture.

_____

_____

_____

_____

ONE-WORLD RELIGION

Cecil John Rhodes and his Society advanced the notion of a one-world religion so that the various races of mankind could merge into a homogeneous whole. To further this development, the House of Rockefeller established the World Council of Churches and promoted the use of form criticism within America's leading seminaries so that ministers and teachers of religion would come to believe that the four gospels are based on mythological events. In keeping with the effort to unite all religious bodies, mainline churches throughout the United States are now engaged in promoting Chrislam, a union of Christianity and Islam. Over seventy-five churches under the rubric "Faith Shared" have initiated a series of month-long sermons and Sunday-school lessons on the teachings of the Prophet Mohammad to bring a common understanding between Christianity and Islam. Along with readings from the Old and New Testaments by Christian prelates, Islamic clerics have been called upon to recite surahs from the Quran.

34

THE NEW NETWORK

1. With the fall of Saigon, the CIA set its sights on the Golden Crescent, where the highlands of Afghanistan, Pakistan, and Iran all converge, for a new source of drug revenue. Since the 17th century, opium poppies were grown in this region by local tribesmen and the market remained regional. By the 1950s, very little opium was produced in Afghanistan and Pakistan, with about 2,500 acres in both countries under cultivation.

Central Intelligence Agency
The CIA got what it wanted. The holy war had begun. For the next decade, black aid—amounting to more than $3 billion—would be poured into Afghanistan to support the holy warriors, making it the most expensive covert operation in US history.

2. The major problem for the CIA was the Afghan government of Noor Mohammed Taraki, who sought to eradicate poppy production in the border regions of the country that remained occupied by radical Islamic fundamentalists.

3. The fundamentalists spurned such efforts not only because of their desire to keep the cash crops but also because they viewed the Taraki government as *shirk* (blasphemy). By 1975, the tension between government and the fundamentalists erupted into violence when Pashtun tribesmen mounted a revolt in the Panjshir valley north of Kabul. The tribesmen were led by Gulbuddin Hekmatyar, who became the new darling of the CIA.

4. Thanks to Hekmatyar's actions, heroin production rose from 400 tons in 1971 to 1,800 tons in 1979.

5. In September 1979, Taraki was killed in a coup organized by Afghan military officers. Hafizullah Amin became installed as the country's new president. Amin had impeccable western credentials.

6. After the coup, Amin met regularly with U.S. embassy officials, while the CIA continued to fund Hekmatyar's rebels in Pakistan. Fearing a fundamentalist U.S.-backed regime at its border, the Soviets invaded Afghanistan on December 27, 1979.

7. For the next decade, black aid—amounting to more than $3 billion—would be poured into Afghanistan to support the holy warriors, making it the most expensive covert operation in U.S. history.

8. The holy war in Afghanistan, in the view of the U.S. geostrategists, offered many benefits, including the possible downfall of the Soviet Union and the possibility of gaining access and control over the vast natural gas and oil resources of Central Asia.

9. The concept of democracy and freedom could never galvanize the scattered tribes and peoples of Central Asia. The people could only be unified by the cause of Allah since they were overwhelmingly Islamic.

10. Months before the Soviet invasion in 1979, the CIA launched Operation Cyclone, an attempt to destabilize the Soviet Union by spreading militant Islam throughout the central Asian republics. Eventually, this operation would serve to create hundreds of Islamic terror organizations, including al-Qaeda.

11. In 1972, the Bank of Credit and Commerce (BCCI) was set up in Karachi by the CIA as a laundry for the drug money.

12. The BCCI became registered in Luxembourg and soon mushroomed into a vast criminal enterprise with 400 branches in 78 countries, including First American Bank in Washington, D.C., the National Bank of Georgia, and the Independence Bank of Encino, California.

13. Virtually free from scrutiny, the BCCI engaged not only in money laundering but also arms trafficking on a grand scale.

14. The enormity of the bank's operations was evidenced by its transfer of $4 billion in covert aid to Iraq from 1985 to 1989. For the Iraqi transfer, the BCCI made use of the Atlanta branch of Banca Nazionale del Lavoro (BNL), an Italian bank with ties to the Vatican Bank. Henry Kissinger sat on BNL's international advisory board, along with Brent Scowcroft, who became President George H.W. Bush's National Security Advisor.

15. After the BCCI went bust in 1991, leaving a financial hole of $13 billion, it came under the scrutiny of the Kerry Commission.

16. By 1982, the "Golden Triangle" of Afghanistan, Pakistan, and Iran was producing 80 percent of the world's opium supply.

17. In keeping with the policy of false flags, the sharp rise in heroin production was blamed on the Soviet generals in Kabul.

18. Western Arkansas suddenly became a hub of international drug smuggling. Drugs were being smuggled into the small airport in Mena by CIA assets, including pilot Barry Seal. These assets also transported to Mena huge bails of cash, which was laundered by BCCI's First American Bank. First American was a Washington, D.C. financial institution that had been acquired for BCCI by former Secretary of Defense W. Clark Clifford. The cash came from the Gambino crime family which was shelling out $50 million for each shipment.

19. The great jihad in Afghanistan grew in scope and strength, threatening to sap the USSR of its strength and resolve. The inhabitants of the five republics of the Soviet Union (Kazakhstan, Kyrgyzstan, Tajikistan, Turkmenistan, and Uzbekistan), who shared a common Turkish heritage and remained devoutly Islamic, became supportive of the *mujahideen* in the struggle against their communist overlords. This support, combined with the massive number of Muslim recruits to the great jihad from the Arab world, served to create a creeping sense of futility among the Soviet troops. To drive the "evil empire" to the point of total collapse, the CIA continued to infuse the holy war with munitions and money, until the war in Afghanistan became the Agency's most expensive covert undertaking.

20. By 1980, the CIA began to send hundreds of militant Muslim missionaries, all members of the radical *Tablighi Jamaat,* to the U.S. mosques in order to call upon young black men to take up arms in the holy war to liberate their Muslim brothers.

21. Sheikh Mubarak Gilani, one of the first of these missionaries to arrive, convinced scores of members of the Yasin Mosque in Brooklyn to head off to guerilla training camps in Pakistan with an offer of thousands in cash and the promise of seventy *houris* in seventh heaven, if they were killed in action. The cash came from the CIA's coffers.

22. Realizing that it would be financially advantageous to train the new recruits on American soil, Sheikh Gilani, with the help of the CIA, set up paramilitary training camps in rural areas throughout the country, including Islamberg in Hancock, New York.

23. To provide more support for the *mujahideen*, the CIA used Abdullah Azzam, Osama bin Laden's mentor, to set up a cell of al-Qaeda within *Masjid al-Farooq* on Atlantic Avenue in Brooklyn, New York. The cell, known as the al-Kifah Refugee Center, acted as a front for the transference of funds, weapons, and recruits to Afghanistan. Throughout the 1980s, this militant organization received over $2 million a year and *Masjid al-Farooq* became a very wealthy institution.

24. In 1980, the CIA deployed Dewey Clarridge, its top agent in Latin America, to establish ties with Honduran drug lord Juan Matta Ballesteros, who operated SETCO, an airline that was used for smuggling drugs into the U.S.

25. By 1990, more than 75 percent of all the cocaine entering the U.S. came through Mexico. Mexico also became a leading source of heroin, marijuana, and methamphetamines. The business was generating $50 billion a year and the CIA had found a source of funding to augment its ongoing drug trade.

DISCUSSION

A. Discuss the distinction between the Golden Triangle and the Golden Crescent.

_____

_____

_____

_____

B. Why was the Golden Triangle of strategic importance to the CIA?

_____

_____

_____

_____

C. Why was the CIA intent upon the removal of Noor Mohammed Taraki from office?

_____

_____

_____

_____

D. Who is Gulbuddin Hekmatyar? How did Hekmatyar gain control of the Afghan poppy fields?

_____

_____

_____

_____

E. Who was Hafizullah Amin?

_____

_____

_____

_____

F. Why did the Soviet Union invade Afghanistan?

_____

_____

_____

_____

G. Discuss the views of Zbigniew Brzezinski on Eurasia.

_____

_____

_____

_____

H. Discuss the plans for the unification of Central Asia and the significance of Turkey.

_____

_____

_____

_____

I. Why was the Bank of Commerce and Credit (BCCI) established in Karachi, Pakistan?

_____

_____

_____

_____

J. Why the need for the BCCI branch offices?

_____

_____

_____

_____

K. Discuss the ties of the Bush family to the BCCI.

_____

_____

_____

_____

L. What was the Kerry Commission? Discuss the Commission's tell-tale findings.

_____

_____

_____

_____

M. How did Western Arkansas emerge as a hub for international drug smuggling?

_____

_____

_____

_____

N. Discuss the ties of Bill Clinton to First American Bank and the importance of this bank to the CIA

_____

_____

_____

_____

O. Why were radical imams dispatched by the CIA to the United States?

_____

_____

_____

_____

P. Discuss Islamberg and the threat posed by the Islamic paramilitary settlements throughout America.

_____

_____

_____

_____

Q. How did al-Qaeda arrive in the United States?

_____

_____

_____

_____

R. What was the significance of Masjid al-Farooq in Brooklyn?

_____

_____

_____

_____

S. Discuss the CIA's ties to the Latin American drug cartels.

_____

_____

_____

_____

THE CREATION OF RADICAL ISLAM

The CIA created the *mujahideen* to ward off the Soviet invasion of Afghanistan and to topple the USSR by the unification of the five Soviet republics in Central Asia under the banner of Islam. To obtain recruits for the holy war against the Soviets, the CIA dispatched radical Muslim missionaries to black communities throughout the United States, since Elijah Muhammad and Malcolm X had initiated the black pilgrimage to Islam.

35

THE GLOBALIZATION OF POVERTY

1. Henry Kissinger was a product of the House of Rockefeller. He graduated from Harvard in 1950 as a Rockefeller Foundation Fellow in Political Science. In 1956, he was invited by the Rockefellers to join the Council on Foreign Relations, where he became a major force in shaping international policy

2. During the 1960s, Kissinger served as Nelson Rockefeller's chief foreign affairs advisor and the mastermind behind Nelson's campaign for the presidency.

Henry Kissinger
Henry Kissinger was a product of the House of Rockefeller. He graduated from Harvard in 1950 as a Rockefeller Foundation Fellow in Political science. In 1956, he was invited by the Rockefellers to join the Council on Foreign Relations, where he became a major force in shaping international policy.

3. When Richard Nixon became president, he appointed Kissinger as Secretary of State in accordance with advice of the Rockefeller family. In this position, Kissinger tirelessly advanced the agenda of the money cartel, including the promulgation of free trade between all nations.

4. This agenda prompted him in July of 1971 to visit China, where he negotiated a trade agreement by which the Communist country would receive "most favored nation" status with the United States, a status that would permit Chinese goods to flow into America free of charge.

5. Manufacturing plants sprouted up throughout China. The products and goods were produced in these plants by workers making less per month than union workers in America were making per hour.

6. Throughout America, factories began to relocate to Southeast Asia and an ever-increasing number of American workers found themselves on the unemployment line.

7. The economic situation in America worsened as more countries, including India and Pakistan, received most favored status. By 2010, fifty thousand manufacturing plants in America had shut down. Almost everything that Americans purchased came from overseas manufacturers: shoes, clothes, cars, furniture, TVs, appliances, bicycles, toys, cameras and computers.

8. On January 1, 1995, the World Trade Organization (WTO) came into being with headquarters in Geneva, Switzerland. It was set up to integrate nations into a world order without tariffs or other economic barriers. The principal beneficiaries were the 80,000 transnational corporations with account for two-thirds of the world trade.

9. The WTO represented one of the final steps in the creation of a New World Order. It was empowered under international law to police the economic and social policies of its 164 member states, thereby derogating the sovereign rights of national governments.

10. Just when it seemed that the situation for American workers could not get worse, the North American Free Trade Agreement came into force on January 1, 1994. The agreement was developed by the Council on the Americas, an organization set up by David Rockefeller in 1965. Thanks to this agreement, the U.S. suffered an additional trade deficit of $181 billion and the loss of one million more jobs.

DISCUSSION

A. Discuss Henry Kissinger's ties to the House of Rockefeller.

_____

_____

_____

_____

B. How did China receive the "most favored nation" status?

_____

_____

_____

_____

C. Why is it impossible for the United States to compete with China in manufacturing goods?

_____

_____

_____

_____

D. Discuss the means by which China manipulates its currency.

_____

_____

_____

_____

E. What other countries have received "most favored nation" status? How has the granting of this status impacted the American economy?

_____

_____

_____

_____

F. How has free trade impacted America's defense industry?

_____

_____

_____

_____

G. What is the World Trade Organization (WTO)?

_____

_____

_____

_____

H. How does the WTO advance the creation of global government?

_____

_____

_____

_____

I. How did the North American Free Trade Agreement (NAFTA) come into being?

_____

_____

_____

_____

J. Discuss the negative impact of NAFTA on the U.S. economy.

_____

_____

_____

_____

K. What accounts for the rise in public sector employment throughout the country? How does this development advance the cause of socialism?

_____

_____

_____

_____

PART TEN

AMERICA, NO MORE

PANEL ONE

"We hold these truths to be self-evident: that all men are created equal, that they are endowed by their Creator with certain inalienable rights, among these are life, liberty, and the pursuit of happiness, that to secure these rights governments are instituted among men. We . . . solemnly publish and declare, that these colonies are and of right ought to be free and independent states . . . And for the support of this declaration, with a firm reliance on the protection of divine providence, we mutually pledge our lives, our fortunes, and our sacred honor."
—THE DECLARATION OF INDEPENDENCE[2]

PANEL TWO

"Almighty God hath created the mind free. All attempts to influence it by temporal punishments or burthens . . . are a departure from the plan of the Holy Author of our religion . . . No man shall be compelled to frequent or support any religious worship or ministry or shall otherwise suffer on account of his religious opinions or belief, but all men shall be free to profess and by argument to maintain, their opinions in matters of religion. I know but one code of morality for men whether acting singly or collectively."

ORIGINAL PASSAGE

"Well aware that the opinions and belief of men depend not on their own will, but follow involuntarily the evidence proposed to their minds; that Almighty God hath created the mind free, and manifested his supreme will that free it shall remain by making it altogether insusceptible of restraint; that all attempts to influence it by temporal punishments, or burthens, or by civil incapacitations, tend only to beget habits of hypocrisy and meanness, and are a departure from the plan of the holy author of our religion..."

—"A BILL FOR ESTABLISHING RELIGIOUS FREEDOM," SECTION I[3]

36

THE ROAD TO 9/11

1. Heroin, by the turn of the 21st century, had become one of the world's most valuable resources—a resource that could generate over $100 billion a year in revenue. Without the white powder, there would be no black ops—no means of obtaining control of Eurasia—no way of molding the global economy and political relations.

Taliban
In June 1998, the Taliban struck a deal with Saudi officials to send bin Laden to a Saudi prison in exchange for Saudi support and US recognition of its legitimacy in ruling the country.

2. On January 27, 2000, Mullah Omar and the leaders of the Taliban announced their plans to ban poppy production within the Islamic Emirate of Afghanistan. Afghan opium poppy harvest had grown nearly tenfold from 250 to 2,000 tons during the covert war of the 1980s, and from 2,000 to 4,600 tons during the civil war of the 1990s.

3. Thanks to the Taliban ban, the opium poppy harvest fell from 4,600 tons in 1999 to 81 tons in 2001. The situation had to be addressed by the military/industrial complex in a forceful way. The ban not only brought the CIA's operations to a screeching halt but also caused a mass exodus of poppy farmers from the fertile fields of the Helmand Valley.

4. The situation in Afghanistan had become worrisome to the House of Rockefeller, which had been instrumental in bringing the Taliban to power in 1996. Through the Union Oil Company of California (Unocal), the Rockefellers had arranged to provide the group with weapons and military instructors. This aid had enabled the Taliban to capture Kabul and to oust Afghan president Burhanuddin Rabbani from office.

5. The Unocal gifts of arms and advisors were given with the belief that the Taliban would provide assistance in the creation of a massive oil pipeline that would run from the oil wells of Turkmenistan through the mountains of Afghanistan to the port city of Karachi, Pakistan, on the Arabian Sea.

6. Unocal also planned through its subsidiary Centgas to build another pipeline—this one for natural gas that would follow the same route through Afghanistan. In the great game of geo-economics, the two pipelines represented the integral parts of the plan to gain control of the "stan" countries.

7. The shadow government, under the direction of Standard Oil and the House of Rockefeller, now planned to thrust farther along the 40th parallel from the Balkans through these Southern Asian Republics of the former Soviet Union. The U.S. military had already set up a permanent operations base in Uzbekistan. This so-called "anti-terrorist strategy" was designed to consolidate control over Middle Eastern and South Asian oil and contain and neutralize the former Soviet Union.

8. Realizing its weaker position *vis-à-vis* the United States, Russia joined the Shanghai Cooperation Organization (SCO), which included China, Kazakhstan, Kyrgyzstan, Tajikistan and Uzbekistan. Its membership in the SCO represented Russia's attempt to maintain its economic control of Central Asia.

9. Once they conquered Kabul, the leaders of the Taliban were whisked off in a U.S. military transport to Houston, Texas, where they were wined and dined by Unocal officials, who had hired Henry Kissinger and Richard Armitage (who would become George W. Bush's Deputy Secretary of State) as consultants.

10. Despite such power players, a final agreement was not reached because the Taliban was being pursued by other oil interests, including representatives from SCO.

11. By 1998, the American power elite realized they had to set up a more cooperative government in Kabul. Plans were made to launch a terror attack against America that could be blamed on Bin Laden and the host of Islamic militants that inhabited Afghanistan, including the Taliban. On August 7th, the U.S. embassies in Kenya and Tanzania were bombed. The attack killed 234 people, twelve of them American, and wounding 5,000 more.

12. A key indication that the embassy bombings represented a false flag operation was the involvement of Ali A. Mohamed, also known as Ali "the American" in the bombing. Following the attack, he was labeled as the "point man" who had masterminded the operation. Two years after the blasts, Mohamed was arrested by the American authorities and pleaded guilty to conspiracy to murder. It then came to light that the alleged al-Qaeda bomber had an impeccable U.S. military service record. He had been trained at Fort Bragg, North Carolina, and worked as an instructor in explosives at the John F. Kennedy Special Warfare Center and School until 1989.

13. Ali A. Mohamed had been recruited by the CIA in Cairo, where he was a major in the Egyptian army. He was then a handpicked graduate of Fort Bragg for American Special Forces and he went on to instruct Green Berets in psy-ops and explosives at the JFK School of Warfare, where he received full security clearance.

14. Despite pleading guilty in a New York court in 2000 to conspiracy to murder American citizens, Mohamed has never been sentenced to confinement. There are no records of subsequent court proceedings and his whereabouts, to this day, remain unknown.

15. In August 1998, the dream of Cecil Rhodes came to fruition with the merger of Amoco with BP to create the world's largest oil company. The House of Rockefeller was now united with the House of Rothschild, and the two nations became inextricably bound both economically and politically. Billions of dollars now flowed into joint military industrial interests and such defense contractors as Lockheed Martin, Northrop Grumman, General Dynamics, Boeing, and Raytheon.

16. Britain's new Labor government under Prime Minister Tony Blair now became America's unconditional ally. The two countries, in accordance with William Stead's foresight, would act in tandem during the war on terrorism, with America as the dominant partner.

17. The movers and shakers behind the Anglo-American Establishment, in keeping with Rhodes's vision, would meet in secret at the annual meetings of the Bank for International Settlements and the Bilderberg Conference. They would also gather within the inner sanctum of the Trilateral Commission, an outgrowth of the Council on Foreign Relations that had been established by David Rockefeller in 1973.

18. After the merger of the oil giants, the primary concern of the new power elite was the need to build the trans-Afghan pipeline and the threat to the world economy posed by the Taliban's ban on poppy production. They realized during their clandestine meetings that these problems could only be resolved by the invasion and occupation of Afghanistan and the removal of the Taliban from power.

19. The first step toward fulfilling this objective had been the bombing of the two African embassies which resulted in making the Taliban synonymous with al-Qaeda even though the two groups were sharply at odds. The second step came with the appointment of Hamid Karzai as the head

of the interim government in Kabul. Prior to this appointment, Karzai had acted as a consultant and lobbyist for Unocal in its negotiations with the Taliban and as a CIA covert operator who had funneled U.S. aid to Mullah Omar and his band of radical Muslim students. The final step was the creation of an incident of enormous proportion that would warrant the planned invasion. That incident came on September 11, 2001.

DISCUSSION

A. How did heroin become the third largest global commodity?

B. Discuss the central importance of Afghanistan to the heroin market.

C. What is Unocal? How did it come to play a pivotal part in the war on terror?

D. What was the role of Centgas on the Grand Chessboard?

_____

_____

_____

_____

E. Why did Russia opt to join the Shanghai Cooperation Organization (SCO)?

_____

_____

_____

_____

F. What brought the Taliban to Texas?

_____

_____

_____

_____

G. What was the need for the bombings of the U.S. embassies in Kenya and Tanzania? What proof exists that these bombings were false flag attacks?

_____

_____

_____

_____

H. Discuss the importance of the merger of Amoco and BP.

_____

_____

_____

_____

I. What steps were taken to bring about the invasion and occupation of Afghanistan and the removal of the Taliban from power?

_____

_____

_____

_____

DREAMS COME TRUE

It was not just another idle pipe dream. The brainstorm that Cecil John Rhodes experienced on June 2, 1877 of a world united by free trade, countries without borders, and a global system of government came to fruition on January 1, 1995 with the opening of the World Trade Organization (WTO) in Geneva, Switzerland. The WTO was empowered under international law to police the economic and social policies of its 164 member states, thereby derogating the sovereign rights of national governments. Eleven years after the creation of the WTO, the House of Rockefeller became united with the House of Rothschild with the merger of Amoco and BP. Billions of dollars now flowed into joint military industrial interests and such defense contractors as Lockheed Martin, Northrop Grumman, General Dynamics, Boeing, and Raytheon. Britain's new Labor government under Prime Minister Tony Blair now became America's unconditional ally. The two countries, in accordance with William Stead's foresight, would act in tandem during the war on terrorism, with America as the dominant partner. The movers and shakers behind the Anglo-American Establishment, in keeping with Rhodes's vision, would meet in secret at the annual meetings of the Bank for International Settlements and the Bilderberg Conference. They also would gather within the inner sanctum of the Trilateral Commission, an outgrowth of the Council on Foreign Relations that had been established by David Rockefeller in 1973.

37

THE MYSTERIES OF 9/11

1. The first mystery concerns the collapse of the Twin Towers, which represents the worst structural failure in modern history. The official story from the National Institute of Standards and Technology (NIST), an agency of the U.S. Department of Commerce, is that the impact of the jetliners produced fires that weakened the structure of the two skyscrapers, resulting in a gravitational collapse. Neither jet fuel nor office fires can reach temperatures sufficient to melt steel (2,750 degrees Fahrenheit), much less to bring steel to a boiling point. Thermite is a mixture of iron oxide and elemental aluminum, that when ignited, reaches levels

Dick Cheney
The stand-down order to NORAD had come from Vice-President Dick Cheney, who was safe and secure within a bunker beneath the White House.

between 4,000 to 4,500 degrees Fahrenheit and produces aluminum oxide and molten iron in a volcanic-like display. The presence of this substance among the ruins of 9/11 provided a tell-tale sign that the collapse of the Towers may have been the result of a controlled implosion.

2. The second mystery is the stand-down order. The U.S. military had spent billions developing stealth aircraft—invisible to radar—that could intercept any air attack on the homeland. But on the morning of September 11, 2001, the North American Aerospace Defense Command (NORAD) was oblivious that four jetliners were invading prohibited airspace and headed for central targets, including the Pentagon. Even after the first jetliner crashed into the North Tower at 8:46 a.m., NORAD proved incapable of locating and stopping the second jetliner from crashing into the South Tower at 9:02 a.m.

3. The third mystery lies with the missing rubble. The Twin Towers collapsed in a manner identical with a planned implosion. Such an implosion would have required the use of pyrotechnic substances—traces of which would have remained among the mounds of twisted steel. Yet 185,101 tons of structural steel that should have been subjected to detailed analysis were loaded on trucks and transported to salvage yards in New Jersey, where the steel was cut into fragments for recycling. A substantial amount of this recycled steel was sold at the rock-bottom price of $120 per ton and shipped off to China.

4. A fourth mystery is the finding that an elite group of Wall Street investors purportedly possessed criminal foreknowledge of 9/11, which permitted them to make a windfall from insider trading.

5. A fifth mystery concerns General Mahmoud Ahmad, the head of Pakistan's Inter-Services Intelligence (ISI). Two weeks after 9/11, the FBI confirmed in an interview with ABC News that Mohammed Atta, the ringleader of terrorists who hijacked the jetliners, had been financed from unnamed sources in Pakistan. Following this announcement, several European news agencies were able to confirm that the money had been wired to Atta from Pakistan by ISI officials at the insistence of General Ahmad. Yet, on the morning of 9/11, Ahmad, the alleged "money man," was in Washington, D.C., conferring with top government officials.

6. A sixth mystery is the collapse of building 7—a 47-story skyscraper located at 7 World Trade Center in New York City that was *not* struck by a jetliner, yet collapsed at 5:20 p.m. with little news coverage. The incident was not even mentioned in the official report from the 9/11 Commission.

7. The seventh mystery surrounds the hunt for Osama bin Laden. At eleven in the morning of 9/11, the Bush Administration announced that al-Qaeda was responsible for the attacks on the Twin Towers and the Pentagon. This announcement was made without a police investigation, a statement of guilt by the leaders of al-Qaeda, or any supporting evidence. Bin Laden became the most wanted man in the world. But the hunt was really a scam. Two months before the events of 9/11, bin Laden was a patient at an American hospital in Dubai where he was receiving treatment for a chronic kidney infection. During his stay in the hospital, the al-Qaeda chieftain conferred with the CIA station head. On September 10, 2001, the day before the attacks, bin Laden was back in the hospital—this time in Rawalpindi, Pakistan, where he received dialysis treatments. In all likelihood, he was still in the Rawalpindi hospital on the morning of 9/11.

DISCUSSION

A. Discuss the significance of thermite among the debris of the Twin Trade Towers.

B. What is the North American Aerospace Defense Command (NORAD)?

_____

_____

_____

_____

C. What accounts for the failure of NORAD to respond to the attacks of 9/11?

_____

_____

_____

_____

D. What accounts for the missing tapes of the air traffic controllers who were on duty the morning of 9/11?

_____

_____

_____

_____

E. Why would Vice President Dick Cheney issue a stand-down order?

_____

_____

_____

_____

F. How is Cheney related to the money cartel?

_____

_____

_____

_____

G. What accounts for the missing rubble at ground zero?

_____

_____

_____

_____

H. How did the money cartel profit from 9/11? Who gained the greatest windfall?

_____

_____

_____

_____

I. Who was General Mahmoud Ahmad? Discuss the significance of Ahmad's presence in Washington, D.C. before and after the terror attacks.

_____

_____

_____

_____

J. What accounts for the collapse of Building #7?

_____

_____

_____

_____

K. Was al-Qaeda responsible for the events of 9/11? Why? Why not?

_____

_____

_____

_____

L. Discuss the problems with the hunt for Osama bin Laden.

_____

_____

_____

_____

M. Where was bin Laden hiding? What is strange about his hiding place?

_____

_____

_____

_____

38

WAR WITHOUT END

1. The possibility that America had been subjected to one of the most horrendous false flag attacks in human history is supported by previous incidents.

2. When Saddam Hussein ventured into Kuwait, President George H.W. Bush, a prominent CFR member, became intent upon launching a war against America's old ally. Bush's ties to big oil interests, including Standard Oil, were extensive.

3. Bush and his cabinet began to circulate stories that Hussein had ordered his soldiers to enter Kuwaiti hospitals in order to remove babies from incubators and to cast them on the floor to die.

Saddam Hussein
Despite the fact that Saddam Hussein was dragged from a hole, placed on trial before a kangaroo court, and lynched, no ties between the Iraqi ruler and al-Qaeda were ever substantiated.

4. On January 14, 1991, Bush launched the Persian Gulf War, which, as it turned out, wasn't much of a war. Within a matter of days, the Iraqi air force was obliterated, along with airfields, missile sites, and communication centers. Throughout Iraq, most means of modern life were destroyed. All electrically-operated installations ceased to function. Food could not be preserved. Water could not be purified. Sewage could not be pumped away. Nine thousand homes were destroyed or damaged beyond repair.

5. Following the war, economic sanctions were placed on Iraq, which resulted in a shortage of medical supplies and food. Malnutrition and disease increased at an alarming rate. By 1998, nearly one million Iraqis, mostly young children and the elderly, had died because of the embargo.

6. In 1999, President Bill Clinton ordered the U.S. Air Force, under the auspices of NATO, to conduct a bombing campaign that reduced Kosovo to a mound of rubble. Between March 24th and June 10th, 37,465 missions were flown, destroying every stronghold of the Christian Serbs.

7. The bombing was justified, Clinton and his administration argued, because the Serbs were committing genocide by murdering thousands of Muslim Albanians for the sake of ethnic cleansing.

8. Since Kosovo was part of Yugoslavia, Clinton blamed Slobodan Milosevic for the alleged atrocities and compared the Yugoslavian president (much in the same manner that George H.W. Bush spoke of Saddam Hussein) to Adolf Hitler.

9. Stories surfaced in the *New York Times* and the *Washington Post* about a massacre in the small village of Racak, where the bodies of Muslim Albanians were left to rot in the street. Another widely-circulated story used to justify U.S. intervention concerned a mine in Trepca, where thousands of bodies of Muslim Albanians were allegedly dumped. Neither story was true.

10. To aid in their struggle for independence, the Muslim Albanians turned to bin Laden and the *mujahideen.* By 1995 more than 6,000 holy warriors from Chechnya, Egypt, and Saudi Arabia had made their way to the Balkans in preparation for the war against the Christian Serbs.

11. Bin Laden visited the area three times between 1994 and 1996 to establish al-Qaeda training camps throughout the Balkans. He also shelled out $700 million to establish the Kosovo Liberation Army (KLA). The purpose of this organization was to drive the Christian Serbs from Kosovo, to topple the government of Slobodan Milosevic, and to unite the Muslims of Kosovo, Macedonia, and Albania into the Islamic Republic of Greater Albania.

12. President Clinton, along with Secretary of State Madeleine Albright, Secretary of Defense William Cohen, and CIA director George Tenet (all CFR members), praised the KLA as "freedom fighters." In no time at all, millions of U.S. dollars were flowing to the Muslim rebels. The United States was now in league with the terrorist group that was purportedly intent upon its destruction.

13. In the wake of the war, more than 200 Christian churches and monasteries in Kosovo were put to the torch. Of the 200,000 Serbs who lived in Kosovo before the war, only 400 were left when the conflict came to an end.

14. After the Christians had been purged from Kosovo, the Pentagon established Camp Bondsteel on the border of Kosovo and Macedonia. This massive military base came to house over 6,000 U.S. troops. The purpose of the camp was to protect the Balkan route whereby heroin flowed from Afghanistan via Turkey to Western Europe, and the Trans-Balkan pipeline which was to channel Caspian Sea oil from the Bulgarian Black Sea port of Burgas to the Adriatic. The feasibility study for the pipeline had been drafted by the engineering division of Halliburton.

15. In 2003, President George W. Bush and his CFR cabinet proclaimed that Saddam Hussein was now in league with al-Qaeda and planning an attack on American soil that would eclipse the events of 9/11. This news was repeated over and over again on 532 separate occasions by Bush and members of his administration.

16. The news wasn't true. No weapons of mass destruction had been found. No plans to develop nuclear bombs had been made. No biological laboratories were fabricating sinister germ warfare. The laboratories that Bush declared the U.S. invading forces had found turned out to be innocuous facilities that were manufacturing hydrogen for weather balloons.

17. The invasion was launched to create a strategy of tension within Iraq. This allowed Anglo-American big oil companies under control of the money cartel to seize Iraqi oil fields and to further their control over the world's supply of energy.

18. In 2011, when Islamic extremists took up arms against the government of Muammar Gaddafi in Libya, the U.S. national news outlets, in tandem with the CFR Administration of President Barack Obama, announced that the Libyan ruler was planning the mass murder of men, women, and children in Benghazi to cower the populace into submission. Therefore, Libya had to be bombed to smithereens for the sake of humanity.

19. Of course, it wasn't true. On March 17, 2011, Gaddafi announced to the rebels in Benghazi, "Throw away your weapons, exactly like your brothers in Ajdabiya and other places did. They laid down their arms and they are safe. We never pursued them at all." Subsequent investigation revealed that when Gaddafi regime forces retook Ajdabiya in February 2011, they did not attack or kill any innocent civilians. The Libyan ruler also attempted to appease protesters in Benghazi with an offer of development aid before finally deploying troops in an attempt to end the rebellion.

20. The Libyan Islamic Fighting Group, the organization of the rebels who opposed Gaddafi, was closely associated with al-Qaeda. Secretary of State Clinton and President Obama were well aware of this fact before they deployed bombers and troops to topple the Gaddafi government.

21. Gaddafi's independence from big oil and the money cartel was the cause of his demise. Earlier in life, Gaddafi's goal was to organize Arabs as a bloc that could withstand Western demands and depredations.

22. Gaddafi also used Chinese energy companies to develop Libya's energy resources, bypassing the interests of the Anglo-American big oil and banking establishments. The power elite, already upset with Russian presence in the Mediterranean, became faced with Chinese presence as well.

23. Evidence exists that the Islamic State of Iraq and Syria (ISIS) was created by the Obama Administration, the CIA and the U.S. State Department under Hillary Clinton. Its purpose, sources allege, is to perpetuate a state of "endless war" that will serve to exhaust Saudi and Iranian military resources; to bring about the dissolution of Syria and Iraq; and to collapse the Arab countries into small states that can be manipulated by the U.S.-dominated money cartel, which seeks control of their natural resources. This thesis is supported by classified CIA documents which affirm that arms for ISIS came, compliments of the U.S., from the arsenal of Muammar Qaddafi.

24. As a result of the endless wars without borders, the citizens of the United States became stripped of the liberties, once viewed as God-given, by the Patriot Act of 2001.

DISCUSSION

A. What threat did Saddam Hussein pose to the money cartel by his invasion of Kuwait on August 2, 1990?

_____

_____

_____

_____

B. How did President George H.W. Bush justify launching the Persian Gulf War?

_____

_____

_____

_____

C. What were the effects of the Persian Gulf War on Iraq?

_____

_____

_____

_____

D. Discuss the economic sanctions that the George H.W. Bush Administration imposed on Iraq and the effects of these sanctions on the Iraqi people.

_____

_____

_____

_____

E. Was Saddam Hussein really a killer of Kuwaiti infants? Why? Why not?

_____

_____

_____

_____

F. Why did President Bill Clinton order the U.S. Air Force to conduct a series of bombing campaigns that reduced Kosovo to rubble?

_____

_____

_____

_____

G. Discuss the Racak and Trepca "massacres." What proof exists that these massacres ever took place?

_____

_____

_____

_____

H. What is the Kosovo Liberation Army?

_____

_____

_____

_____

I. How did the United States become allied with al-Qaeda during the war in the Balkans?

J. What were the real reasons for the war in Kosovo?

K. Discuss the reports from President George W. Bush and his administration that Saddam Hussein possessed weapons of mass destruction that he planned to unleash against the American people.

L. How were these reports discounted?

M. What was the real reason for the invasion of Iraq?

_____

_____

_____

_____

N. What charges did President Barack Obama level against Muammar Gaddafi?

_____

_____

_____

_____

O. How were these charges unmasked as mendacities?

_____

_____

_____

_____

P. What were Gaddafi's crimes against the money cartel?

_____

_____

_____

_____

Q. Was the Islamic State of Iraq and Syria (ISIS) created by the Obama Administration? Why? Why not?

_____

_____

_____

_____

R. What is the covert purpose of ISIS?

_____

_____

_____

_____

S. Discuss the ramifications of the Patriot Act.

_____

_____

_____

_____

THE END OF LIBERTY

As a result of the endless wars without borders, the citizens of the United States became stripped of their liberties, once viewed as God-given, by the Patriot Act of 2001. No longer did they possess freedom of association. The government now could monitor religious and political institutions without suspecting criminal activity to assist terror investigation. No longer were they granted freedom of information. The government closed once-public immigration hearings, secretly detained hundreds of people without charges, and encouraged bureaucrats to resist requests for the disclosure of public records. No longer did they possess freedom of speech. The government could prosecute librarians or keepers of any other records if they told anyone that the government was seeking information related to a terror investigation. No longer did they retain a right to legal representation. The government could monitor federal prison jailhouse conversations between attorneys and clients and deny lawyers to Americans accused of crimes. No longer were they free from unreasonable searches. The government could search and seize their belongings, including their personal papers, without probable cause for the sake of a terror investigation. And no longer were they granted the right to a speedy and public trial. The government now could jail anyone, including its citizens, without a trial on charges of terrorism.

39

AFTER THE FUNERAL

1. The uniqueness of Rhodes resided in his insistence that the process of globalization could be controlled by a "synarchy"—an elite group of bankers, businessmen and industrialists, who meet in secret to chart global affairs.

2. Rhodes believed that the process of history—a process that Marx called "dialectical materialism"—would result not in the formation of the "stateless state" but rather a socialist system in which the vast majority of mankind would become dependent upon big government to provide their basic needs.

3. Among the original members of Rhodes's Secret Society, the most influential was Nathan Rothschild, who set up the House of Morgan to control the economic development of America. The Rothschilds would give rise to the Pilgrim Society within New York's Waldorf Astoria Hotel that was off-limits to the general public. Within this rarified setting, the wealthiest men in the country could meet to shape national policy.

4. The House of Morgan served as the driving force behind the creation of the Federal Reserve System, which would control the country's money supply and the prevailing interest rate. This central bank was privately owned by representatives of the world's leading banking consortia: Morgan, Rockefeller, Rothschild, Warburg, and Kuhn-Loeb.

5. These families represented a classic cartel. A cartel is a group of independent businesses which join together to coordinate the production, pricing, or marketing of their members. In the case of the Federal Reserve, these elite families became joint shareholders who worked together to manipulate the U.S. and world economy. They possessed the ability to create depression or prosperity.

6. The banking cartel, under the leadership of the House of Morgan, manipulated events, including the sinking of the *Lusitania*, which brought America into World War I for the purpose of creating a global government.

7. At the onset of the Great Depression, the interlocking interests of the cartel gave rise to the establishment of the Bank for International Settlements (BIS) in Basel, Switzerland, where the banking families met in absolute secrecy. These meetings resulted in the creation of a covert economy based on real wealth, that is, gold. At the outbreak of World War II, the Rockefellers emerged as the dominant family within the cartel. Through the efforts of this family, the United Nations, the World Bank, the International Monetary Fund (IMF), and the World Trade Organization came into being. These organizations worked in tandem to dissolve the sovereignty of the United States.

8. Rhodes's dream of a world unencumbered by tariffs or any barriers to free trade, thanks to the cartel, had become a reality. While labor remained stationary, capital moved. America's mighty manufacturing plants were relocated in the Third World, where workers were plentiful and willing to labor long hours for a pittance. Goods were no longer made in America, but in such places as China, Japan, Indonesia, Africa, the Philippines, and Mexico.

9. As America lost its industrial base, its citizens became more and more dependent upon the government to meet their basic needs, including health care. Democracy, in accordance with the plan of Rhodes and his Secret Society, had dissolved into socialism.

10. American workers—once the most productive and well-paid labor force in the world—became forced to submit to the increasing demands of globalization and the money cartel. Their wages dwindled; their benefits all but vanished; and their working hours became extended. Two adults in a family had to work—most in the service industry—to make ends meet. The cleft between the haves and have-nots grew to such an extent that the middle class disappeared into the widening fissure.

11. Those who sought to advance from their insecure positions were advised to seek higher education. But the cost of tuition climbed to such an astronomical level that the average student graduated from college over $100,000 in debt.

12. While the working class suffered, and the infrastructure of America's cities fell into ruins, the money cartel continued to seize natural resources throughout the world in order to sustain their hegemony. Such seizures required conflict, and Americans, by tens of thousands, began to die in limited wars that were fought not for freedom but the economic interests of the chosen few.

13. The same chosen few created the Central Intelligence Agency to topple governments hostile to its interest. These covert operations were funded almost solely by the sale of heroin. The heroin, cultivated and distributed under the auspices of the CIA, came from Southeast Asia, necessitating the Vietnam War, and then Afghanistan, necessitating the "war on terror."

14. When the U.S. military occupation of Afghanistan became precarious, the CIA worked with the Mexican drug cartels to develop poppy fields throughout the mountains of Mexico's west coast.

15. Heroin by the turn of the 21st century had become one of the world's most valuable resources—a resource that could generate over $100 billion a year in revenue.

16. By 2014, $500 billion to $1 trillion in proceeds from criminal activity and black ops were laundered through the world's leading banks—half of which were located in the United States. Narcodollars became the lifeblood of the nation's economy.

DISCUSSION

A. How does the concept of a "synarchy" characterize the vision of Cecil Rhodes?

_____

_____

_____

_____

B. What, according to Rhodes, would be the final result of the process of history?

_____

_____

_____

_____

C. Why did Nathan Rothschild emerge as the most influential member of Rhodes's Secret Society?

_____

_____

_____

_____

D. Discuss J.P. Morgan's ties to the Rothschilds and his role in the creation of the Federal Reserve.

_____

_____

_____

_____

E. What is a cartel? How did a cartel evolve that took control of the U.S. economy?

_____

_____

_____

_____

F. Discuss the leading role of the House of Morgan in the cartel.

_____

_____

_____

_____

G. Why was free trade integral to the fulfillment of the vision of Cecil Rhodes?

_____

_____

_____

_____

H. How did the House of Rockefeller become the dominant power within the cartel?

_____

_____

_____

_____

I. What effects have free trade had on the American worker?

_____

_____

_____

_____

J. Discuss the emergence of the Mexican drug cartels. How are these cartels controlled by the CIA?

_____

_____

_____

_____

K. What is the importance of heroin to the banking industry?

_____

_____

_____

_____

L. Discuss the evolution of the United States into a narcocapitalist country.

_____

_____

_____

_____

EPILOGUE

RAISING THE DEAD

1. The New World Order of the plotters of Uncle Sam's demise would be based on socialism. Events would be manipulated so that the American people would become utterly reliant on the government, which the plotters would control from the shadows. The government, under their direction, would institute free trade, the out-shoring of American manufacturing, and the creation of a global labor force. Wars would be conducted to break down the borders between countries and the free flow of commerce. International agreements and agencies would be established. Uncle Sam would be sapped of his industrial strength.

2. By controlling the news media and the educational system, the plotters would be able to change the way in which Americans viewed reality. The populace would be conditioned to relinquish their cherished beliefs in order to embrace the virtues of diversity and multiculturalism.

3. Uncle Sam's demise progressed in stages. First, they deprived him of his right to manage his own finances. His wealth in gold was stripped from his possession and shipped to a place where it could not be recovered. Swimming in debt that he could not pay, his days of manifest destiny and incredible achievements came to an abrupt halt.

4. Next, they entangled Uncle Sam in foreign affairs and conflicts from which there was no escape. One war led to another with such rapidity that the old man began to lose his grip on reality.

5. Then Uncle Sam was drugged with opiates and his teeth were extracted, since they were well aware that the avuncular figure could bite.

6. The only hope for even a partial recovery of Uncle Sam resides with the initiation of the following series of restorative measures:

7. The first measure is to audit the Fed. While the Fed's financial statements are audited annually, its monetary policy operations remain exempt from scrutiny by the Government Accountability Office (GAO), the investigative arm of Congress. The GAO is currently prohibited by law from examining discount window and open market operations; agreements with foreign governments and central banks; and Federal Open Market Committee (FOMC) directives. It is precisely this information that should be made public. The American people must know how and why Fed officials expand the money supply, set interest rates, and conduct transactions with other central banks and foreign governments. It is not enough for the Fed to simply provide its updated balance sheet after crucial decisions and transactions have been made.

8. The second measure is to produce real money based on precious metals. China has already taken the lead by taking measures to back the yuan with gold. When this goal is accomplished, China will possess the world's most valuable currency and the paper dollars produced out of nothing by the Fed will no longer serve as the world's favored means of financial exchange.

9. The third measure is to end the endless wars. For the most part, the wars serve no interest of national security. Tens of thousands of American soldiers have been killed to advance the hegemony of the money cartel. To make matters worse, the United States has been dragged into these bloody conflicts by lies and acts of deception. The end of the endless war also would enable the U.S. to close its archipelago of 700 to 1,000 military bases in 130 countries and its vast expenditures for the military-industrial complex at home.

10. The fourth measure is the elimination of the CIA. Since its establishment in 1947, the Central Intelligence Agency has operated at the whim of the money cartel to topple governments, institute strategies of tension, and to install strong-arm regimes in countries throughout the world. Their efforts have resulted in the creation of the *mujahideen*, al-Qaeda, and ISIS. Its reliance on drug money to fund its black operations has resulted in the Vietnam War and the War in Afghanistan. Its covert activities undermine national security and drag the United States into costly conflicts—conflicts that only serve to sustain the economic hegemony of the money cartel. The Senate Intelligence Committee cannot control the rogue intelligence agency. The reports of the Committee on the CIA's dirty undertakings are kept "under wraps" and free from public scrutiny on the grounds that they concern matters of "national security." The CIA is compelled to report only to the President, but since Congress exercises control of the budget, it possesses the right to oversee the spy agency's undertakings. It is high time for many of these undertakings to be brought to light and terminated.

11. The fifth measure is the forgiveness of the national debt. Of the $19,850,000,000,000 national debt, over $5.5 trillion is owed to federal agencies. This debt has been incurred by the U.S. Treasury Department's borrowing from the trust fund of one federal agency to give to another. By absolving the debt which the federal government owes to itself and the Federal Reserve, the country will be able to expand the debt held by foreign investors and, thereby, obtain the means to address its rotting infrastructures and to forgive student loans that are albatrosses around the necks of many young Americans.

12. The sixth measure is the cessation of funding to colleges and universities. Student-debt forgiveness must be accompanied by the curtailing of federal and state funding for colleges and universities that fail to provide job placement for their graduates. For the most part, these institutions of higher education fail not only to equip their graduates for employment but also to ground them in the fundamentals of academics.

13. The seventh measure is the investigation of foundations. Throughout the 20th century, the foundations increased their influence over America's educational system until they became the source of 20 percent of the total income of America's private and public colleges and universities. By shelling out hundreds of millions of dollars to boost the administrations and instructional staff of these institutions, they could dictate what courses should be offered and (by providing the funding to develop the textbooks) how such courses should be taught. In this way, they managed to control the thought of America's college students, so they would embrace the tenets of globalism, including the acceptance of diversity as a national virtue. The influence of the tax-exempt foundations expanded past the realm of education to include the once celestial fields of American Christianity. The Rockefeller Foundation gave rise to the National Council of Churches and the World Council of Churches, organizations which campaigned for abortion-on-demand, same-sex marriage, and liberation theology. During the 1950s, Congressmen Eugene E. Cox (D-GA) and Carroll Reece (R-TN) launched an investigation to determine which "foundations and organizations are using their resources for purposes other than the purposes for which they were established, and especially to determine which such foundations and organizations are using their resources for un-American and subversive activities or purposes not in the interest or tradition of the United States." This investigation was brought to a halt by President Eisenhower, whose ascent to the White House was funded by the House of Rockefeller. It's time for the investigation to begin anew.

14. The eighth measure is the downsizing of the government. Absolving the federal debt owed to the Federal Reserve and the federal government must be accompanied by downsizing the federal government, which spends five dollars for every three that it collects in taxes.

15. The ninth measure is the imposition of tariffs. To reduce its dependency on foreign goods, the United States must impose tariffs on all imports and it must use the revenue amassed in this manner to reduce the taxes on goods produced in the United States. Free trade, the religion of Cecil Rhodes, has resulted in the loss of manufacturing plants, which once represented a central source of employment for the American people.

16. The tenth measure is the draining of the swamp. Members of Congress have been corrupted by their dependence on money from lobbyists—and from the special interests hiring those lobbyists—to fund their reelection campaigns. By 2016, the amount spent on campaigns by all candidates for Congress soared beyond $4 billion, with incumbents spending between 30 to 70 percent of their time fundraising rather than legislating. This was all well and good, since the time that they spent legislating was, for the most part, advancing the policies of their benefactors.

17. The eleventh measure is the overthrowing of judicial tyranny. The decisions made by the country's highest court which stand in conflict with the will of the people must be overturned. The judges must be subjected to ten-year term limits and their reign of tyranny must be brought to an end. Congress must attach a rider to every law dealing with social policy that it is not subject to judicial review. And should the Supreme Court continue to act in a dictatorial manner, their rulings should be ignored. This is in keeping with American tradition. Abraham Lincoln in his first inaugural address said: "If the policy of the government upon vital questions affecting the whole people is to be irrevocably fixed by decisions of the Supreme Court … the people will have ceased to be their own rulers, having to that extent practically resigned their government into the hands of that eminent tribunal."

18. The twelfth measure is the advancement of states' rights. The polarization of the United States into a nation with conflicting moral, political and spiritual ideologies can only be resolved by the reversal of power from the federal government to states, cities, and towns, so that the citizens of various regions of the country could resolve their own problems in their own way and in accordance with their own principles. This development would be in accordance with the long-forgotten 10th Amendment of the Constitution which stipulated: "The powers not delegated to the United States by the Constitution, nor prohibited by it to the States, are reserved to the states, respectively, or to the people."

19. The thirteenth measure is a halt to immigration. Such a measure is not incongruous with U.S. history as witnessed by the restrictive immigration measures of the 1920s and the imposition of a quota system. The halt on immigration must be accompanied by a correct interpretation or a repeal of the 14th Amendment, which permits any child born to an illegal alien or foreign visitor on American soil to become automatically a U.S. citizen.

20. The last measure is another Great Awakening. Americans no longer share the same history and heritage. Not even the same European roots or common language. But, for the most part, they share the same religion. In 2017, over 70 percent of the inhabitants of the United States identified themselves as Christians. The vast majority—even those who rarely, if ever, darkened the doorway to a church—continued to share the same faith and to worship the same God as the American forefathers. This faith can be rekindled by the winds of revival. Such a monumental spiritual event has happened twice before on American soil.

DISCUSSION

A. Discuss the stages of Uncle Sam's demise.

_____

_____

_____

_____

B. What can be accomplished by an audit of the Federal Reserve?

_____

_____

_____

_____

C. Why must the United States produce real money? What are the dangers of fiat money?

_____

_____

_____

_____

D. What can be accomplished by a weakening of the Federal Reserve?

_____

_____

_____

_____

E. Why must the United States put an end to endless war?

_____

_____

_____

_____

F. What is the purpose of the 172 U.S. military bases in Germany? Why have bases been established in Aruba and Australia?

_____

_____

_____

_____

G. How did the CIA become a rogue agency? Discuss the need for covert operations.

_____

_____

_____

_____

H. How can the national debt be absolved?

_____

_____

_____

_____

I. Discuss the failure of America's colleges and universities to ground students in the fundamentals of academics.

_____

_____

_____

_____

J. Do the institutions of higher education throughout the country require or merit federal funding?

_____

_____

_____

_____

K. Should America's private foundations be subjected to investigation? Why? Why not?

_____

_____

_____

_____

L. What measures must be taken to downsize the federal government?

_____

_____

_____

_____

M. Discuss the effects of foundation funding on America's educational system.

_____

_____

_____

_____

N. How have the foundations impacted the realms of religion and morality?

_____

_____

_____

_____

O. Discuss the Reece Commission. Why did Present Eisenhower halt its proceedings?

_____

_____

_____

_____

P. Discuss the imposition of tariffs and the dangers of international free trade.

_____

_____

_____

_____

Q. How can the swamp in Washington, D.C. be drained?

_____

_____

_____

_____

R. Discuss judicial tyranny and how it can be overthrown.

_____

_____

_____

_____

S. What is the 10th Amendment? Discuss the importance of states' rights.

_____

_____

_____

_____

T. Why is a moratorium on immigration required?

_____

_____

_____

_____

U. How can the people of the United States be reunited as nation?

_____

_____

_____

_____

V. Discuss the 1st and 2nd Great Awakenings.

_____

_____

_____

_____

A LINEAR PLOT

Nathan Rothschild, William Stead, and Lord Archibald Primrose (Rothschild's son-in-law) were prominent members of the Secret Society that had been created by Cecil Rhodes to forge a New World Order under British rule. They recruited prominent American industrialists—including Andrew Carnegie, J.P. Morgan, and John D. Rockefeller—to their cause. Morgan set up a chapter of the Pilgrim Society in New York's Waldorf Astoria Hotel. The setting was apt since William Waldorf Astor, the owner of the hotel, was closely related to Rhodes and Rothschild. Within the rarified setting of this hotel, Morgan, Carnegie and the wealthiest men in America opted to commit their enormous resources to shape national policy, to effect an Anglo-American alliance, and to bring the vision of Cecil Rhodes to full fruition. Morgan and his fellow "pilgrims" became the driving force behind the creation of the Federal Reserve System, which would control the country's money supply and the prevailing interest rate. This central bank was privately owned by representatives of the world's leading banking consortia: Morgan, Rockefeller, Rothschild, Warburg and Kuhn-Loeb. A money cartel was formed to gain control of the world's true wealth, its natural resources. Other secret societies, under the direction, of the cartel were formed, including the American Roundtable, the Council on Foreign Relations, and the Trilateral Commission. By lies and acts of deception, America was dragged into war and foreign entanglements that would serve to break down borders, create mass immigration, and open an international marketplace without trade restrictions. Under the governance of the cartel, America would be stripped of its sovereignty and its uniqueness as a nation. Eventually, the cartel would fall under the control of the House of Rockefeller, which would give rise to the United Nations, the International Monetary Fund, the World Bank, the World Trade Organization, the globalization of war, and the globalization of poverty. Thanks to changes in immigration legislation, the floodgates of America would be open to Third World invaders and the country would lose its distinctive race and religion. Who killed Uncle Sam? The correct answer is Mammon.

NOTES